PARANORMAL PA

ED KELEMEN

DEDICATION

This book is dedicated to our honorary daughter, Kathleen Henderson, the brightest light in any room. She brings her enthusiasm and positive outlook to everywhere she visits and everyone she meets.

Table of Contents

Dedication

Table of Contents Continued

ACKNOWLEDGMENTS

Thanks to Bob Frank for the use of his picture of the smoking pipe to illustrate the haunting at Mr. Ed's home in Ortanna, PA.

And, of course, thanks once again to Linda Ciletti for yet one more of her incomparable cover illustrations that perfectly complement and enhance the contents of this book. She is truly a graphic artist without peer.

And a shout out of thanks to the Ghost Research Foundation for taking me in, teaching me about the paranormal, and allowing me to partake in investigations and wonderful fellowship. You guys are outstanding!

Foreword

Welcome to Paranormal PA, a compendium of paranormal activity throughout the Keystone State spanning both time and distance.

These stories have been collected over a period of years from everyday folk, just like you and I.

This book would have been impossible to write without the input of people willing to share their stories. C. William Davis, "Mr. Ed" Gotwalt, Alyssa Raye Taylor, Tom Beck, Warren A. and Bethany M. Mack, Sean and Amy Kelemen, Joanne McGough, Beverly LaGorga, Kathleen Henderson, Carol A. Birney, Brendan Kelemen, and Rhonda Johnson all shared what, for some of them, must have been terrifying experiences. I am equally indebted to those other witnesses who, for one reason or another, wish to remain anonymous.

These shared stories are of extraordinary events witnessed and experienced by ordinary people, most of whom didn't believe in the validity of such events. That is, until they witnessed them for their own selves. Paranormal activity can, and will, take place at any time of the day or night, in areas of quietude and in places crowded with people.

Read on and, above all – enjoy.

What is Paranormal?

Paranormal is an adjective, "denoting events and phenomena that are beyond the scope of normal scientific understanding." That's what the world authority on word usage, the Oxford Dictionary, has to say about it. It goes on to say, "There is a great deal of information in the ancient Vedic texts on paranormal phenomena."

If you can read and understand ancient Sanskrit script, knock yourself out and enjoy delving into what was written by Hindi scholars some 3,000 to 3,500 years ago. I'm going with the Oxford Dictionary.

In my research, I was cautioned about lumping Paranormal and Supernatural together. That's because one school of thought contends that, while *paranormal* events are outside of current scientific knowledge, some day those events will be within the scope of scientific reasoning. On the other hand, *supernatural* events are outside the scope of natural occurrence altogether and will never be understood scientifically.

I disagree because the very concept of never is an anathema to me. What today is commonplace scientific knowledge was considered supernatural as recently as a century ago. How arrogant could I be to say that what we don't understand now will never be understood?

So, within the confines of this book, *paranormal* will be defined as that which is outside the scope of both current scientific understanding and that which is outside the scope of what the average person understands as normal.

This includes hauntings, apparitions, ghosties, ghoulies, and things that go bump in the night.

At least one governmental cover-up of a UFO crash in the woods of the western part of the state is described.

There are also stories about cryptids. What is a cryptid? Simple, it is just an animal that has yet to have been captured and quantified by mainstream scientists. For instance, for hundreds of years, the coelacanth was deemed to have suffered extinction during the end of the Cretaceous Period with the dinosaurs. That is, until one was captured live in 1938, and another in 1997. Until the ceolacanth was actually captured live, its sightings were dismissed by scientists as folklore and it was relegated to the ranks of cryptozoology. Cryptozoology is the study of creatures whose existence is disputed or unsubstantiated. Examples of cryptids include Bigfoot, crypto bird, and canid sightings.

But the great majority of events depicted between these covers involve otherworldly events in the realm of the afterlife.

And this brings us to our next question ...

What is a Ghost?

Some other words for ghost are: apparition, bogie, familiar spirit, haunt, hant, haint, materialization, phantasm, phantom, poltergeist, shade, shadow, specter, spirit, spook, sprite, vision, visitant, and wraith, to name a few in alphabetic order.

But that doesn't tell us what a ghost *is*. For that we will go ask Merriam Webster, who says a ghost is a disembodied soul; especially the soul of a dead person believed to be an inhabitant of the unseen world or to appear to the living in bodily likeness. The word comes from the Middle English *gost* or *gast*, and from the Old High German *giest*. Its first known use was before the 12th century.

Those of us who consider that death is simply a transition and not an end consider a ghost to be nothing more than the continuation of a living person's essence after his or her corporeal body has ceased to function. (That's a nice way of saying *died.*)

Ghosts are just people like you and I. And like people, ghosts have many personalities, moods, and character traits. Some are nice, some are average, and some are nasty. There are times they want to be left alone and there are times when they are a bit more gregarious and are willing to interact. And, just like people, I've found that treating ghosts with respect gets their respect in return. Remember the magic words: *please* and *thank you.*

Why are they here on the corporeal plane of existence? Why haven't they transitioned to the next plane of existence, the afterlife, Heaven, Valhalla, Hades, the Elysian fields, Loka, the Happy Hunting Grounds, or whatever you chose to call it?

Because, for one reason or another, they have unfinished business here. Perhaps they have a compelling message to deliver to someone who is important to them. Sometimes a person has suffered such a violent, trauma-filled death that they don't even know they have passed on. Other times, their death has been so swift they haven't realized it has happened.

Some are satisfied with existence on this side and have decided they don't *want* to cross over. They're having fun *here,* so why go *there*? The ghosts of children are often in this category.

Some feel their life on the earthly plane has been less than exemplary and are resisting crossing over lest they wind up in an overly warm place. Hell, Tartaros, Naraka, and Gehenna come to mind.

Some are being held here against their will after running afoul of other denizens of the dark: one of the greatest reasons to avoid playing with Ouija Boards.

Hauntings

Now, when any of these ghosts, spirits, or whatever you want to call them frequent a location, it is said to *haunt* that location. The location is said to be *haunted.*

Two main kinds of hauntings are *residual* and *active.*

Residual hauntings are the ones where a person cannot interact with the spirits. This is because the spirits as they appear are not really there, or are not aware of being there. This happens at places where such strong emotions and/or traumatic events have taken place that the very area is imprinted with them. When an observer encounters one of these hauntings it is as though he or she is watching a movie on an endless loop. The event is simply playing and replaying, over and over again.

In Pennsylvania, a good example of this kind of haunting happens at the Gettysburg National Battlefield. People frequently see spirits of soldiers, both Union and Confederate, in and out of formation, participating in the battle. However, they can only observe the spirits. They cannot interact with them because those spirits aren't really there. It is a representation of part of the battle that has been actually imprinted on the battlefield. When conditions are right, they become visible.

Examples of two other residual hauntings are at the location of the former *S. S. Grandview Ship Hotel* on US Route 30 in Juniata and *Dead Man's Curve*, also on US Route 30 just a few miles east of Laughlintown.

At the S. S. .Grandview location you can sometimes hear the sounds of diners enjoying their meals in the restaurant of the former hotel. But that's all you can do. You can hear them, but you can't interact with them.

Likewise, at the location of Dead Man's Curve halfway up Laurel Mountain east of Laughlintown, the sounds of out-of-control trucks racing down the slope can be heard as the drivers struggle to regain control. Roaring engines, air brakes, and horns all join in to predict the inevitable crash to come. Then they fade as quickly as they came, leaving you with a rapid beating heart and nothing else. There will be no crash. You have just heard what was imprinted on that fateful curve by unfortunates who have come there before you. Sometimes they made it through and sometimes not.

Active hauntings occur when you the observer, and the spirit are aware aware of one another and can communicate. A couple of examples of active hauntings that can be found elsewhere in this book are *The Quirky Little Haunt* and *Spirits from the Little Church on the Hill.*

Apparitions

How does a ghost or spirit make itself known? The name of the game is *energy*. These manifestations use energy, energy that the spirit doesn't have. This energy has to come from an external source. Just like our TV sets won't work unless and until we plug them into an outlet for energy; a spirit can't make himself or herself known unless there is energy available to do so.

Electrical energy is a great and readily-available source inside occupied buildings That's why lights often flicker when a spirit makes itself known.

Other sources include flowing water, which provides tremendous energy. Less than a foot of flowing water in a stream has enough energy to wash a full-sized vehicle downstream. The vicinity of electrical transmission lines is another good source. And batteries. All those batteries that we bring to a paranormal investigation provide a lot of energy for the spirits. *The Mystery of the Recharging Batteries* gives some insight into this phenomenon.

Manifestations range from those using the least amount of energy to those using the most amount of energy.

At the low end of the energy scale are *orbs* or *ghostly spheres.* Personally, I tend to discount orbs that show no evidence of motion. That's because so many other things can be mistaken for actual orbs. Especially things like dust motes and pollen. To lessen the appearance of these anomalies, care should be taken to take pictures without flash. Another test to verify them is to watch for intelligent movement. That is movement that cannot be explained by outside interference such as air currents.

Next are EVPs (Electronic Voice Phenomenon). EVPs occur when a paranormal investigator is equipped with a digital voice recorder and then goes into an area suspected of being inhabited by spirits. Setting the recorder to "record," the investigator then asks the spirit questions, leaving a long pause between questions for answers. Upon playback the recorder may have answers to the investigator's questions or other messages entirely. These are called EVPs. The spirits use the power in the recorder's batteries as a power source to be able to respond in this manner.

Next up the scale are amorphous mists congregating and congealing in an area. These are sometimes called protoplasm and are in varying stages of transparency. These are the most common of actual apparitions and resemble a transparent bed sheet, or a mist that resembles tobacco smoke. In both of these instances, the apparition is unaffected by wind currents.

Requiring more power are partial apparitions. These appear as portions of a human body, transparent and colorless. It can be the head, the head and torso, the torso, the upper or lower extremities, or a combination of these parts. It will be easily recognizable as a human or animal form.

The most power-consuming of appearances is the full-body apparition. A human form appears, once again in stages of transparency from misty to opaque, but most often semi-transparent. The ubiquitous "Lady in White" falls into this category.

Many times, in this book and others, the Lady in White is mentioned. She has been seen in every possible paranormal context. She appears at the side of the road hitch-hiking. She is seen floating in various places and circumstances. The Lady in White walks into a lake and disappears under the merciless waters. She rides along with you in your car only to fade from view as her destination is approached. She flits about cemeteries. She stands alongside and in the middle of roads, next to fences, peers from windows and doorways, and is generally the most seen phantasm.

Are all these appearances of The Lady in White, the same spirit? Of course not.

It takes a tremendous amount of energy for a spirit to manifest itself materially.

It requires much more energy than most spirits have at their command to appear as a full-bodied apparition. That's what makes full-bodied apparitions so rare. That energy has to come from somewhere and that's why apparitions are accompanied by cold spots. Heat is a form of energy, and it is the most readily-available one. By draining the heat in an area, a spirit can increase his or her available energy, then use that energy to interact with us.

A full-bodied, three dimensional appearance is one of the most energy-draining events that a spirit can accomplish. By appearing in a semi-transparent, monochromatic state the interaction can last longer to achieve the spirit's intent. This monochromatic event is usually in shades of gray, like a black and white photograph. Within gray scales, all light colors appear as though they are faded white. So, female spirits wearing dresses are often assumed to be wearing white dresses when they appear, thus promulgating the legend of "The Lady in White."

The second most energy draining manifestation of a spirit is a full-color, full-body apparition. These are exceeding rare and I know of only one that has been captured photographically. And that is at the Ligonier Tavern in Ligonier.

What is the most energy draining way for spirits to interact with us? By exerting physical force to move inanimate objects.

Let's start this journey with a love story ...

Rosie and Mac

A Love Story Beyond Death

Farmland Near Altoona, PA

Rosie waited for Mac to come home. It was late, she had already put the two little ones to bed. It wasn't like him to be late. Mac always tried to schedule his week so that he left the big rig at the depot early enough to be home for supper come Friday night. There was never a lot of money, but she always tried to have something special for his Friday night dinner, the first home cooking he would get since Sunday afternoon.

She didn't realize how much she missed him until it got close to the time for him to be home. She absolutely loved it when he burst through the kitchen door, swept her off her feet and smothered her with kisses as he spun her around. Then he spoiled the girls with whatever gifts he was able to pick up on his weekly five night over-the-road journey. It was never anything big, just something so that they knew he thought about them while he was away. They adored their daddy.

Likewise, she adored her husband, companion, lover, protector, confidant, and anchor.

After the girls settled down and went to sleep, she cleared the table, wrapped the food, and put it away so it wouldn't get stale. Someting must have happened, but it would turn out alright. It always did. There was the time he got stuck in a snow storm in Montana for four days. She remembered once he got diverted back to Texas and missed an entire weekend at home. Then there was when the truck broke down in Vermont and he had to wait for repairs to be done. He'd call whenever he got to a phone.

She sat alone at the kitchen table chain-smoking and drinking tea. Life wasn't easy in the Allegheny Mountains for a twenty-three year old mother of two married to an over-the-road truck jockey. They were just starting out in life in a six room fixer-upper on 10 acres. Not much, but better than the cramped 3 room apartment they had in town before he got on with the trucking company.

She thought of their song, the one Patsy Cline sang on the radio,

"Oh, we ain't got a barrel of money,

Maybe we're ragged and funny.

But we'll travel along

Singin' a song

Side by side."

She drifted off to sleep right at the table with her head cradled in her forearms, the song still echoing in her mind,

"I don't know what's a'comin' tomorrow

Maybe it 's trouble and sorrow

But we'll travel the road

Sharing the load

Side by side."

As she slept, she entered dreamland and her husband came to her in that state, standing right at her side next to the kitchen table. "Baby." That was his favorite nickname for her. He always said that if Lauren Bacall could be Bogie's baby, she could be his.

"Baby – wake up. I need to tell you some things."

She rubbed the sleep from her eyes and looked up at him. He wasn't wearing his regular big smile. He looked downright serious.

"Wha- what's the matter hon?" She asked.

"Nothing Baby. I just want you to know that you're going to be alright."

"I know that, silly. I have you to take care of me."

He shook his head from side to side. "No Baby, this is serious. I want to tell you some things."

She nodded and he went on. "My life insurance policy from the trucking company is in the bureau drawer with all my important papers. And the military life insurance that I took out when I got discharged is with it. Between the two of them there is over $40,000. Plus, I took out loan insurance on our mortgage, so the house and property will be paid off. Got it?"

She nodded again and said, "Honey, what's wrong. You're scaring me."

He shushed her and said, "I don't have a lot of time to finish this, so I need you to listen. If you're careful with it, the money from the insurance should last you and the girls until you get the farm up and running. And I don't want you to spend a lot of money on the funeral..."

She interrupted, "What funeral?"

"Baby, please just shut up and listen. I don't want buried in no fancy duds, just some clean blue jeans and my favorite green flannel shirt. I never wore a suit and tie in my life and I sure don't want to wear 'em for eternity."

She was speechless as the import of his conversation dawned on her. He went on, going so far as to tell her exactly what casket he preferred (the cheapest one). "... and don't let no mealy-mouthed undertaker switch you into something more expensive. It don't matter if I'm buried in a casket made of wood or in one of gold, it's all the same to me." He told her who he wanted for pall bearers and who he thought would give the most honest eulogy, "the Lord knows I weren't no saint, so don't make me out to be none."

Wide eyed with just the hint of tears starting to form, she nodded again.

Like I said, Baby, you're going to be alright." And with a kiss on the tip of her nose, he faded from sight.

"Through all kinds of weather

what if the sky should fall?

As long as we're together

It doesn't matter at all."

The raucous ringing of the phone intruded on her dream.

She snatched it from its cradle and answered it saying, "Honey, I just had the strangest dream about you. Wait'll I tell you about it."

But it wasn't him. It was her mother-in-law.

"Rosie, your phone's been out of order or something. People've been trying to get you for over an hour. Get up and get dressed. Mac's been in an accident. The hospital called and said we have to get there as soon as we can. I'll pick you up in 20 minutes."

"Did ... did ... did they say if it was serious?" she stuttered.

"Yes, they said it is serious."

>*<

People commented on how composed she was making arrangements and tending to all the details of the funeral. If she wept at all, it was in private.

When both the undertaker and her in-laws balked at burying Mac in jeans and a flannel shirt, she stood her ground, saying, "It's what Mac told me he wanted."

Same thing when some of the relatives felt they would be more appropriate pall bearers than the ones chosen.

"Take it up with Mac," she said.

>*<

Forty-five years have come and gone and Rosie never remarried. She raised their girls and now has a flock of grandkids and a smattering of great-grand-kids to spoil. And the final verse of the song sometimes wafts on the night air while she drinks that last cup of tea before bed,

"When they've all had their quarrels and parted

We'll be the same as when we started

Just travelin' along

Singin' a song.

Side...by...side."

And she smiles.

Granny in her Rocker

Butler County, PA

An older fellow related this one to me:

"I'm from Butler County here in PA and have been for all my life. Same with my wife. Let me tell you something that happened a few years ago.

"It was in the late 1990s or thereabout and my wife's momma had taken ill, so we went over to her house a lot to care for her. One particular day I had worked all day cutting firewood and was just about completely tuckered out.

"Well, you see, her mom lived in the old family home on the family farm that had been in the family for generations. It went back to before the Civil War. It was a big ole two story frame thing with add-ons and covered porches and all.

"That particular day when I was dog tired, we went over to help out as best we could and make her mom comfortable and bring her some food. If I remember right, she had a touch of some kind of flu or something. Anyhow, while the missus was upstairs tending to her mom, I decided to relax on the couch downstairs. I think I had the TV on, but I don't remember that for sure.

"I must've drifted off to sleep, cause the next thing I knew, I was woke up by the sound of the old rocking chair creaking back and forth on the wood floor over by the front window.

"I rubbed my eyes and looked over there and saw a really old lady just rockin' back and forth, back and forth, smiling and looking out the window. She was wearing a dress with a apron and a little cloth covering her hair.

"I called over to her to see if I could help her or something and, right before my eyes, she disappeared, just like that! She looked at me, smiled and faded away.

"I ran upstairs to my wife and mother-in-law and told them all about it.

"They told me not to worry about it, it was my wife's grandmother's favorite chair and she still likes to rock away in it from time-to-time."

The Gibson Girl Comes Home

Tarentum, PA

C. William Davis III, Bill to his friends, is an author and speaker of some renown. His mystery series featuring Clive Aliston, a no-nonsense sheriff who solves unsolvable crimes in and around the gritty manufacturing center of the Steel City, Pittsburgh, has received both critical acclaim and popular success.

In 1974 Bill moved his family into what was once one of the more affluent areas of East Tarentum, PA and took possession of a comfortable home on East 6th Avenue.

A bit after they moved in, he became aware of a seepage problem in the basement. Not wanting to bear the expense of a major project replete with backhoes, cement trucks, and so on, he decided to fix it himself by diverting ground water away from the foundation. This was a labor intensive solution, but it did save quite a bit of money.

One day, while he was cutting sod and digging at the back of his home, his shovel struck an object that gave off a slight "clink" sound when it was hit. He got down on his hands and knees and retrieved an ancient blue glass bottle with its cork intact. It even contained some residue of its original contents.

A short while later, a nearby elderly neighbor engaged him in some friendly conversation and happened to notice the bottle.

"You know what you've got there?" he asked

"A really old glass bottle," Bill replied.

"Not just that, but it is a Laudanum bottle and still has some in it. Do you know what Laudanum is?"

Bill replied that, if he remembered correctly, it was an opium mixture that was used for a large number of ailments in the 19th and early 20th centuries.

"Right you are!" the old fellow said. "You've got a good find there. Maybe it's worth some money to a collector."

And the conversation headed off in a new direction. They discussed things like the weather and the demise of the steel industry in the valley and so on.

Eventually the neighbor asked him if he noticed anything unusual about his house.

"Like what?" Bill asked.

"Oh you know. Things out of the ordinary, weird things, strange lights, and so on," The fellow replied.

"Why do you ask?"

"Well, before you bought the place, it was empty for quite a while. From time-to-time, when the wife and I were sitting on our back porch in the evening we saw lights flickering and moving back and forth inside the windows on the second floor. It was at night when we knew there was nobody supposed to be there."

"We've heard some sounds and things moving about at night, but we just figured it was the normal sounds of an old house settling in. Why?"

"You don't know the history of your home, do you?"

Bill confessed that he didn't and his neighbor asked him if he had ever heard of Evelyn Nesbit, the world's first super model.

"Just a little, from the movie that was made about her in the 1950s," was his reply.

"Well Bill, Florence Evelyn Nesbit spent most of her childhood in that very same house. She was born Christmas Day 1884 or 1886 in another part of town. Then, when her father became more wealthy, the family moved into that house and stayed there until 1893.

Even as a baby and toddler, her beauty brought her fame and people would come from all around just to gaze on the face of this beautiful child. It was the happiest time of Evelyn's life with two doting parents who strived to see that she wanted for nothing.

In 1893, with the increased success of her father, an attorney, the family moved to Pittsburgh. But he died shortly after the move and left the family penniless. Her mother decided to capitalize on Evelyn's beauty. and she was "discovered"

She became the first number one super model in the world before her 16th birthday. Her face and body adorned everything from playing cards to magazine covers. Her name was known in every household in the country as the most beautiful woman in the world. It started when she became a dancer in the chorus line of a Broadway show and was suddenly "discovered" by famous pen and ink artist Charles Dana Gibson. Before she knew it, she was in featured roles along the Great White Way and added the title of "Broadway Star" to her resume. She found herself wooed by millionaires and international stars alike, from the fabled John Barrymore to ultra-rich New York Architect Stanford White. All this for the little girl from the small industrial town of Tarentum, PA that had a population of 4,000.

On top of it all, she was just 16 years old to hear her mother tell it. Some accounts said that she was only 14.

That's what Florence Evelyn Nesbit faced in 1901. After a lavish courtship, she was plied with champagne and lost her virginity to 47 year old Stanford White, called "Stanny," by his associates. He then passed her on to a friend of his, actor John Barrymore, who was 21 at the time. Smitten by her beauty and being an honorable man, he asked for her hand in marriage. Based on the advice of her mother who considered Mr. Barrymore's financial future as an actor to be uncertain, she turned him down.

Then she met Pittsburgh multimillionaire Henry Thaw and subsequently married him in 1905. Instead of an idyllic existence free from financial cares, she found herself a virtual prisoner in the Thaw Mansion, called Lyndhurst, on Beechwood Boulevard in the Squirrel Hill section of the city.

Henry Thaw was obsessed with his wife's past showing symptoms of what today would be called paranoid schizophrenia fueled by a morphine addiction. On June 25, 1906, Henry Thaw and his young wife Evelyn attended a rooftop production of *Mam'zelle Champagne* at the Madison Square Garden. Also in attendance at a private table was Stanford White. During the closing production number, "I Could Love A Million Girls," Henry Thaw approached Stanford White. Standing less than three feet away, he shot White three times in the head, obliterating his face.

Standing over Stanford White's dead body waving his pistol in the air, Henry Thaw addressed the crowd, shouting, "He ruined my wife!"

What followed was a media frenzy and a courtroom sideshow that was called, "The Trial of the Century," the first of many given that appellation. Judged criminally insane, Henry Thaw was sentenced to an asylum in upstate New York. After seven years, his wealth managed to get him judged sane and he walked out a free man. He died in 1947 leaving his wife $10,000 of his $1,000,000+ estate.

The movie, *The Girl in the Red Velvet Swing,* released in 1955 and starring Joan Collins, Ray Milland, and Farley Granger was based on her early life and marriage. She served as technical adviser for the movie and received a few thousand dollars for it.

Evelyn finally passed on in 1967 after a career that never approached her earliest fame.

And that is what Bill learned about the unfortunate Evelyn. It seemed as though his home was the home of a famous celebrity's spirit who wanted to stay where she remembered her favorite time. Or at least the old man said so.

As years passed, Bill and other members of his family heard unexplained noises from time-to-time, one corner of the dining room was always as cold as the inside of a refrigerator, even in the summer, and the sweet smell of lilacs would waft on the air when there were no flowers present.

Bill learned that lilac was Evelyn's favorite flower and wore perfume of that aroma.

Hmm, Bill thought when these things would happen, *Maybe the old fellow has something after all.* Then he'd give his head a negative shake and return to reality.

The family cat had no problem believing. He'd arch his back, extend his fur to twice its regular size, then spit and hiss at something or someone no one else could see.

Bill's family grew and his daughter Michelle matured into a beautiful young woman herself, attracting the attention of local young men. One in particular, Heath, became her steady beau and was a household fixture, accepted as one of the family.

One evening in particular, when the hour grew late, he asked for permission to sleep over, rather than head home at such an hour. Bill readily gave him that permission, with one caveat: he had to sleep on the couch in the downstairs living room while Michelle slept upstairs in her own room. Satisfied with the arrangement, the family settled down, the home grew quiet, and everyone surrendered themselves to the spell of Morpheus, Greek God of Dreams.

In the morning, as the family gathered round the kitchen table for breakfast, Bill asked Heath how he enjoyed his sleep on the couch.

Came the answer, "The couch was comfortable enough, but I will never sleep another night in this house!"

"Why so?" Bill asked.

"Well," he told him, "Everything was fine at first. The couch was quite comfy and I settled in for a nice night's sleep. But some time around 3 or 4 in the morning, I woke up. I don't even know what woke me, just something.

"Anyhow, I sat up and looked around to see what it was that woke me. I looked over to the stairs leading up to the second floor and saw a young lady walk down the stairs to the landing. She paused on the landing and I saw that she was wearing a long filmy nightgown of some sort or another.

"I thought it was Michelle and called out to her, but she didn't answer. She just continued down the stairs, and walked down the hall to the kitchen.

"I guessed that Michelle didn't hear me and was going into the kitchen for a middle of the night snack or something, so I followed her there. When I got to the kitchen, it was empty. Nobody was there. And nobody left the kitchen, either, I would have known.

"It must've been a ghost or something and I will never spend another night in this house!" he repeated himself with emphasis.

Ruminating on the event later, Bill remembered his old neighbor's conversation word for word as though it had just happened. He and the rest of his family had been accepting the strangeness of the house until the day they moved in 2004.

He wondered if maybe, just maybe, the guy was right after all.

ED KELEMEN

Premonition, prediction, or clairvoyance?

Saxonburg, PA

One afternoon at a book signing, I was approached by an elderly gentleman who introduced himself as Max and said that he thought he might have, "ESPs." Since I know at least one certifiable genius who can't pronounce the word "serif" properly, I found no humor in his misuse of the word.

With a little prodding, he told me what had happened to him and his family one day a few years back.

Max had a beautiful daughter by the name of Marcelline who was blessed with someting sorely lacking in a lot of today's youth – a work ethic. Instead of spending her free time chained to a game console, an MP3 player, or sending endless texts on an iPhone, she went out and got a job.

Since she was a high schooler, it was a minimum-wage job at a local fast food restaurant where she spent a lot of time flipping burgers and making fries.

"Marci would always tell me that maybe it only paid minimum wage, but it was a lot more than she would get for sitting on the couch watching TV," Max said.

Nevertheless, every night when she came home from her shift, she would spend a long time in the shower getting the smell and feel of grease from her hair and off her body.

I could see Max's pride in his daughter when he told me that, from time-to-time, he would chide her for using too much water or shampoo. It was a private joke between the two of them.

One evening Max fell asleep watching TV. He usually didn't do this, but he had had a tiring day at the loading docks. So, after dinner he plunked himself in his recliner and had a beer while scanning the day's headlines in the paper. Even though it was a morning paper, Max preferred to read it at night.

Well, by and by, Max nodded off and the paper fell to his lap.

Max didn't remember falling asleep or dreaming anything for a while. Then he had a nightmare. He heard his Marci screaming over a vat of hot grease that had splashed her face when she put a batch of fries into it. The nightmare faded and didn't awaken him.

He was awakened by the sound of the telephone on the stand next to his recliner. And he knew who it was before he even answered it.

"Hello."

"Mr. --------, do you have a daughter named Marcelline?"

"She's been burned hasn't she? What hospital is this? I'm on my way."

As things worked out, Marci wasn't burned badly, just a few spots on the side of her face and her left ear. And they healed nicely without even leaving a scar.

The only question that Max had was to ask me, "If I had wakened earlier, could I have saved my little girl the pain she went through?"

I confessed that I didn't know, but probably not. I told him that he was probably witnessing it as it happened and he couldn't have done anything about it.

I don't know if that was the right answer, but it made both of us feel a little better, and isn't that what it's all about?

The Guardian

Pittsburgh

During late October 2016, I was at an event produced by Mandi Pryor of MP Marketing and hosted by Wigle Whiskey Barrelhouse and Whiskey Garden in the North Side of Pittsburgh. The event was called "Whiskey and Words."It was a book fair, sale, and signing by over a dozen of the area's authors, myself included. The Mary Ann Mangini trio provided the perfect mood-setting music for the event with the trio's namesake chanteuse heating up the evening with her sultry take on songs of the 40s and 50s.

While there, I had the opportunity to renew old friendships and make some new ones. One of the new ones that I was able to make was with inspirational speaker and author Carol A. Birney.

As is often the case with me, our conversation turned to the realm of the paranormal, hauntings, ghosts and the like.

And she related this little story to me:

When Carol was a young lady in her early twenties, just starting out on life's grand adventure, she found, fell in love with, and moved into an older house that was to become her home for many years. The original owner had recently passed away and she was able to get it from his estate at a good price.

One night, shortly after moving in, she retired to her bed for the evening. After a bit, she got the feeling that she wasn't alone. She sensed a presence. Not a malevolent presence, but rather a calming one. So, she sat up in bed and looked around the room, the only illumination provided by a low wattage night light. When she looked to the foot of her bed, she saw an elderly gentleman standing there. He posed no threat and was just sort of looking down on her the way a protective father might look upon one of his children. And, after a bit, he just kind of faded from sight.

Instead of being frightened, she felt a reassurance in his presence. And his appearances became an almost nightly ritual. She would go to bed. After a while, he would appear, watch approvingly over her for a bit, and then disappear.

She investigated and learned that the former occupant of the house had two daughters and it was his practice to stop in each of heir bedrooms every night to make sure that they were OK before he himself would retire for the night. Perhaps, after his death and Carol's subsequent occupation of the house, she became his surrogate daughter whom he felt compelled to watch over.

In any case, after a few years, Carol met the love of her life who shortly thereafter became her husband. On the day that her husband moved into the house, Carol's protector disappeared, never to be seen again. Perhaps he felt that Carol's care was now in more capable hands so he passed the responsibility on to those hands.

Hairy Chests, Missing Money, and Pink Kitchens

Swissvale, PA

After years of hospice nursing, author Joanne McGough retired from the hectic city life in and around Pittsburgh. She now resides in beautiful Laughlintown, Pa at the foot of Laurel Mountain with her collies, Tanya and Rocky and the feline boss of the house, Daisy. When not composing cozy page-turners like *A Bed and Breakfast Affair*, she spends time doting over her children and grandchildren, as well as tending her flowers and catching up on her traveling and cooking.

As a young wife and mother, Joanne lived in a stately, 100-plus year-old Gothic style frame house in the Pittsburgh suburb of Swissvale. Her family grew and the house was filled with the joyful sound of young girls playing, running up and down the stairs, and just generally getting into those things that youngsters are apt to.

That's about the time she noticed that things had a way of disappearing in the house. Nothing important, mind you, but it was a minor irritation. Things like keys, bobbins and needles, grocery lists, and so forth. And these things never stayed missing for an extended period of time. They always showed up in a while, but usually someplace other than where they had last been seen. Joanne always attributed these happenstances to a faulty memory or to someone else in the home moving them and then forgetting about it. No big thing, but mildly aggravating just the same. In addition to things being moved about, Joanne also had an uneasy feeling that she was being constantly watched in her own home, even when she was supposedly the only one there.

Brendan was the family's big ole friendly Irish Setter who had been named after Brendan Behan, the famous Irish Republican author. Now he had taken to raising his hackles and growling at a particular corner in the living room when nobody was in that corner.

One day, Joanne placed fifty dollars in the form of two twenties and a ten in a drawer. It was to buy groceries. Fifty dollars back in those days wasn't exactly considered chump change.

Imagine her consternation when she returned to retrieve the money and it was gone. This time it was no memory slip or inadvertent misplacement. It was theft, pure and simple. She questioned her husband thinking he might have needed it for car repairs or some such. Nope, he had nothing to do with the missing money. Likewise, the girls all expressed denial and no knowledge of the money's whereabouts.

The missing money was a blow, but life went on and she put it out of her mind, only remembering it occasionally.

The following summer she decided that the house was in need of a complete cleaning, top to bottom. Part of that included removal of the carpets to send them out for cleaning. When the carpet was rolled up in the room where the money had gone missing, fifty dollars consisting of two crisp twenty dollar bills and one ten dollar bill were lying smack dab in the middle of the floor that the carpet had covered. Numerous pieces of furniture had had to be removed to roll up that carpet and it wasn't within the ability of any one single person to do it.

It was the missing fifty dollars, no doubt

about it. That's when Joanne realized that someone or something other than living human beings was sharing the house with her family. And she was going to do something about it. She called in a reader.

When Joanne mentioned the petty and sometimes not so petty thievery that had been going on for the past year or two, the first thing the reader asked was, "Are there any young girls in the home?"

When Joanne told her about her young daughters, the reader told her not to worry. Oftentimes, when girls are maturing into young women, they attract the attention of just such an imp as has been making his presence known by moving things about. It isn't really anything evil, it just wants attention. It'll go away as the girls grow a bit older.

Then she went on, "What about the big man with the hairy chest?"

"Big man with a hairy chest? Don't know what you're talking about," Joanne replied, but then remembered that uneasy feeling of being watched.

"Oh yes, there is the spirit of a large man with a hairy chest in this house. I get the impression that he is either the previous owner or the builder of this house. He isn't malevolent, he just wants to make sure that his house is being taken care of properly."

When Joanne later mentioned this to her husband, Ed, he said, "Oh yes, I've seen him a couple of times in the upstairs hallway. And one time he was standing alongside the bed just looking at me."

Joanne wanted to know, "Why didn't you tell me?"

Ed told her, "I didn't want to scare you."

Back to earlier that day when the reader continued, "But I wouldn't worry about anything here anyway. You're not going to be living here that long."

"Huh?" was all that Joanne could muster as way of reply.

"I get the feeling that you or your husband is going to inherit a new home. I see red brick and particularly, a pink kitchen."

Sure enough a scant year later, a relative of her husband passed away leaving them a brick duplex. And when Joanne entered what was to be their new home for the first time, she was struck by the clean and tidy *pink* kitchen.

A HOUSE OF DEATH

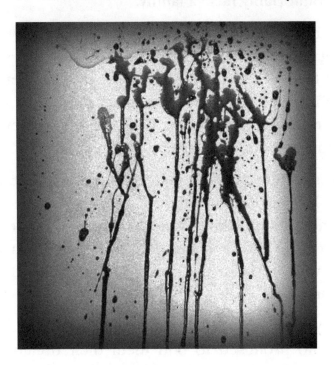

Suburban Washington County

The young couple was starting out, but neither of them were naive. He was a Navy veteran who had continued his education after his discharge and was now in middle-management in his chosen field of computer engineering. She was a tenured grade school teacher who was well-liked by students, family, and faculty alike. This was a couple destined for success, both professionally and personally.

After a year or so of marriage, they decided that they

wanted to settle into a home of their own where they could comfortably raise a family.

There were a few requirements for their new home. They planned on having some children to express their mutual love, brighten up their lives, and complete their little family unit. So the new home had to have a bit of "elbow room." A large yard was a necessity so they could enjoy the outdoors and not be cramped.

Location was another consideration. He didn't want her to have a long commute to work, since he was concerned about winter weather driving conditions in western PA. It wasn't as much of a problem for him, but he did want to keep his back-and-forth work travel to under an hour.

They gave their list of requirements to a real estate agent who promised to find them their dream home. But, after a few weeks of looking, they were starting to despair of finding their personal Shangra Li.

Then they got the call from the agent who said, "I think I've found your new home. It has everything you want and it's located in a quiet neighborhood to boot."

The tree-lined street where the house was located looked like a suburban paradise. Well kept lawns fronted immaculate homes and even a close scrutiny revealed no drawbacks. They parked in the driveway listening to the real estate agent prattle on about all the amenities of the home and the neighborhood: new appliances, landscaped front and rear yards, wrap-around redwood deck, the Jacuzzi in the master bath, vaulted ceilings, nearby swim club, access to upscale shopping in the area, and on, and on, and on.

They weren't really paying attention, they were absorbing all they could about the beautiful house on its huge lot. They were favorably impressed as they exited the car and followed the agent to the house. The agent unlocked the front door and stood aside so that they could fully appreciate the magnificent entryway and foyer.

The young wife stepped into the slate floored foyer and looked around. The interior was as beautiful as the exterior. But she didn't see all the results of the wonderful interior decorating that went into the home. What she saw was a haze of red. What she felt was a miasma of horror and death. Nearly sick to her stomach with fear, disgust, and an overwhelming sense of death, she stumbled back to the car. She made her apologies to the real estate agent, blaming her nausea and lightheadedness on a touch of possible food poisoning.

After she was alone with her husband, she confided in him what she had really felt in that house.

"Honey," she said, "I can only say that that place somehow told me that it was a house of death."

And, with no further discussion, they turned down the deal on what the real estate agent called their "dream house." It was more of a "nightmare house" to them.

Only later did they learn that it was indeed a house of death. A particularly gruesome murder had taken place in the master bedroom of this seemingly benign domicile.

The young wife had been warned away by someone, or something from the misunderstood beyond.

A Haunting in Brownsville

Brownsville, PA

Brownsville, PA is situated on a bluff overlooking the Ohio River near the first ford of that river for people heading westward from the mountains of Pennsylvania. Small wonder then, that it is located at the juncture of three main Indian trails.

It was first settled by whites in 1785 after the "pacification" of the Iroquois tribes allowed resumption of westward immigration by settlers. In that year, a trading post opened overlooking the river to serve those immigrants. That little trading post, owned and operated by John Bowman, expanded into a tavern and inn to further serve those people and the town began a rapid expansion. In fact, John and his family did so well at that site that he built a home there that was called Bowman's Castle at first, then Nemacolin Castle after the western terminus of the Indian Trail of that same name.

Brownsville evolved from a trading post to an outfitting and marketing center, then a transportation hub, riverboat building powerhouse, and industrial nexus. During the 1800s Brownsville was *the* place to go for Steamships, providing over 3,000 of the river-conquering craft during that time. Up until the 1850s when the Baltimore and Ohio Railroad was completed, Pittsburgh was forced to live in Brownsville's shadow. With the completion of that railroad, along with the discovery that Pittsburgh was ideally situated for the manufacture of iron, then steel and glass, Brownsville began a slow decline in importance. During it's first century and a half of existence Brownsville was understandably a raucous place along the bank of the Ohio.

As such, it gathered its own fair share of haunts and hauntings with the castle on the bluff being home to ten spirits of its own.

But, I'm not writing about the more famous haunts of the town. They have been fairly documented to the point that those spirits have almost become celebrities. No, I am writing about a haunt that brought fear to a family.

Late in 2016 I had occasion to be at an event in Greensburg that was attended by well over 200 persons. One of those persons, a middle-aged family man, approached me and asked if I had ever been frightened by a ghost.

I replied, "Startled, even shaken – yes. But frightened – no."

I went on to explain that the only things that actually frighten me from the other side are demons and poltergeists. Spirits, haunts, ghosts, whatever you want to call them, are merely people who have gone on to another existence. If you treat them with respect and understanding, they will reciprocate. Up to this point in my life, I have yet to encounter a powerful poltergeist. Demons have to be invited before they can enter from the other side and I am not about to do that.

He said that, nevertheless, he and his family have a terrifying experience with a ghost in his house. Here, allow him to tell it in his own words:

"My home is built along one of the Indian paths that meet in Brownsville. It's really nothing special, not too old and not too new. It really hasn't been around long enough to acquire a ghost, if you know what I mean.

"It's a split-level style with the garage and basement on the lower level and the living areas on the upper level. My family and I have always been happy there.

"Then came *that day*.

"My ten year-old daughter had gone down to the basement area for something and wander into the garage.

"Suddenly, she let loose the most horrible, terrified scream I have ever heard in my life.

"I rushed to the steps leading down to the basement and garage pushing, knocking, and kicking things out of my way.

"As I got halfway down the stairs, I saw a woman in my basement. She was wearing a dress like those that the ladies wear for those ren-fests, if you know what I mean."

I nodded and he went on.

"She gave me such a look of utter hatred that I was chilled clean through, then she turned and disappeared through the concrete block wall of the basement.

"I ran to my daughter who was standing in the middle of the basement, too terrified to even move. She just stood there, rooted to the spot shaking like a leaf. I swept her up in my arms and carried her up to the living room, telling her all the while that everything would be OK.

"When she calmed down, I was able to talk with her about her experience. She told me that, when she went to the basement. she couldn't find what she had been looking for; so she went to the garage to see if it was there.

"In the garage she saw the lady in the back of my pick-up truck, in the bed. But she only saw the top half of her. It was like the bottom half went right through the floor of the truck bed to the ground. She could tell that the lady hated her for some reason and wanted to hurt her. When the lady came towards her, she ran into the basement, but she couldn't go any farther. All she could do was to scream. And that's when she saw me coming down the stairs and the lady walked through the wall.

"I asked her if there was anything unusual about the lady and she said that yes, the lady was wearing a pendant.

"What was special about the pendant, I asked her and she replied that it kind of shined real bright like and was a funny shape.

"I asked her about that and she couldn't describe it, but offered to draw it. When she drew the pendant, it was a six-sided star, like the Star of David.

"This event shook the entire family and we held a prayer session there and have been fortunate enough to have never seen that lady again."

"What do you make of that," he asked me.

I confessed that I had a couple of theories, but no real answer and advised him to burn a bit of white sage in his basement and garage and to keep praying.

ENCOUNTER ON
TURKEY HILL MOUNTAIN

Somerset County, PA

Don't let Bethanie Mack's beauty you. Just because she has intrinsic beauty and a sense of compassion that exudes comfort and caring doesn't mean that she can't kick butt when necessary. Certain people who confused kindness with weakness found this out the hard way. This transplanted farm girl is equally at home in an evening gown as well as well-worn jeans. These days, however, she prefers to stay at home in a sweatsuit cuddling on the couch with her husband Warren.

As a teenager, Beth loved the outdoors and spent as much of her free time as possible exploring rural Somerset county on her single-seat quad-runner. One of her favorite rides was through the woods of the Stoystown area and up the flank of locally-named Turkey Hill Mountain. Once at the mesa on the top, she loved to look out over the never-ending rolling vista of Pennsylvania's tree covered hills and mountains.

On one outing, then sixteen year-old Beth was accompanied by a group of friends, six in all. Besides her quad, there was a pair each of quads, 3-wheelers, and dirt bikes. The group rode the single track trails to the top of the mountain and paused to rest a bit. They had gotten a late start that day and evening was fast approaching when they submitted the hill. The mountain tops were starting to acquire that light purple haze that makes sunsets in the Pennsylvania highlands so beautiful.

After a bit, Beth noticed a peculiar smell wafting her way and mentioned it to the other riders. She says that she can only describe it as an overpowering combination of sweetness and muskiness combined with a cloying stickiness. She wasn't the only one to notice it. At first the consensus was that a large animal, like a deer, was rotting somewhere nearby. But, these were country kids and they knew what a rotting deer smelled like. This wasn't it. They looked about for the source of the odor and heard some disturbance in the brush a ways downhill. By now, evening had settled in and those who had them turned on their headlights for illumination.

Beth scanned the treeline with her headlights spotting the origin of the smell, and it terrified her. It was an animal-human hybrid of some kind that stood almost eight feet tall. She knew this because it was as high as the branches that she and her friends liked to swing on sometimes.

It was covered head to toe in medium length red fur interspersed with streaks of gray.

When the headlights of the 4-wheelers alighted on it, it turned and gave the group of youngsters a malevolent stare. Beth says she will never forget those deep, black pupil-less eyes that watched her with such hatefulness.

That was enough for her! Beth, possibly the bravest of the whole bunch, was the first one down the mountain to the relative safety of a paved road. She never rode her quad-runner on Turkey Hill Mountain again.

Sasquatch?

Bigfoot?

You be the judge, she's not going back to find out.

The Fayette County Courthouse

North

&

West Faces

South

&

East Faces

Photos Were Both Taken Within 5 Minutes of One Another

Uniontown, PA

From his honored perch high atop the courthouse of the county bearing his name, the Marquis de Lafayette has the best vantage point in Uniontown, PA.

And he has enjoyed the panorama of the valley in this manner since March of 1847. From 188 feet above Main Street he had the best view of anyone of the old county prison jail yard where executions by hanging were carried out until 1914.

So, it is probable that his stern visage was cast upon an unfortunate soul who had been condemned to die. He was scheduled to to hang from his neck until dead on the gallows at the Fayette County Prison in Uniontown, PA as the courthouse bell tolled the noon hour. He was definitely guilty of the crime for which he had been sentenced. The sentence was true and just. He was aware of his guilt and had no argument with any of the proceedings. Except one.

10 minutes before the scheduled execution the prisoner was led up the creaking steps of the gallows located in the jail yard. His feet were placed on the trap door whose opening would end his stay on this mortal coil. The noose was placed around his neck and snugged, but not too tight. He could still speak.

He still had 5 minutes to go before his scheduled end, but the hangman, who possibly had a more pressing engagement elsewhere wanted to speed things up. He asked the hapless condemned man if he has any final words before the trap was sprung.

The prisoner looked up, not to God in heaven, but to the courthouse clock looming over him which indicated that he still had 5 minutes to go. He realized that he still had 5 minutes to go and that he was about to be cheated out of his last 5 minutes of life. He was speechless with rage.

The hangman mistaking his mute rage for a refusal to speak, placed the hood over his head and the executioner's hand reached for the lever. He only had short seconds to make his final statement. What to say?

Did he apologize for his crime that brought him to this terminus? No. Did he curse the judge, jury, and police? No. Did he beg for his miserable life, such as it was? No.

No indeed. Instead of any of those, his voice muffled by the hood, cursed the clock showing him that he was being executed 5 minutes early. He cursed it to forever run 5 minutes slow to atone for those 5 minutes of life stolen from him by the impatient executioner.

In a slightly different version, the prisoner's last statement curses the clock to always show a different time on its four faces.

In any case, the four faces of time on the courthouse tower have never agreed as to the proper time of day, and still do not.

Haunts at the Elks Club

Connellsville, PA

The Connellsville Elks Club is located in a venerable old building located at 140 East Crawford Avenue in the river town of Connellsville, PA. It wasn't always so. It was officially organized as Lodge 503 of the Benevolent and Protective Order of Elks on June 25, 1899. During its early years it was hammered with financial woes and difficulty in raising money. But it was finally able to purchase this building in 1916. It came complete with a bowling alley that members used for over 20 years.

During this intervening century many additions and modernizations have taken place. In 1937 the bowling alleys were sold and the present-day grill room and dining area was installed for members and guests. In 1956 a complete remodeling and modernization was undertaken. This involved demolition and reconstruction and the new digs were rededicated during February 1957. Another round of renovations occurred in 1973, and the Lodge hall and barrooms were rebuilt in 1999.

Over a hundred years of rebuilding, renovations, and remodeling have resulted in the up-to-date facility that Lodge 503 has called home for all these years.

Entering the Lodge via the main entrance on Crawford Avenue, I was confronted with what I call the "Wall of Death." Stretching along most of the left wall and covering a bit of the right wall as well, is an Honor Roll that celebrates each and every member of this Elks Lodge who has passed away after joining the organization. The earliest member deaths go all the way back to the turn of the twentieth century. Over the years, at least two members have passed away on the premises, one of them while seated at the bar on the first floor. It has been said that when you join the Elks, you are a member for life. Well, some members have taken that to extremes and have retained their membership long after their earthly existence has expired. (I wonder how they pay annual dues.)

Right before you get to the Wall of Death, just inside the front door and immediately to the left is a door leading to another room. One wall of that room is covered with pictures. Every one of the Exalted Leaders of the Lodge since its inception in 1899 are represented on that wall. And, standing in front, observing those benevolent visages, you just may encounter what others have – a cold spot indicating that one or more of them are standing there with you.

And this is no wonder. After all, this noble building has existed through two World Wars, the Korean War, the Vietnam War, floods, fires, flu epidemics, polio, and the Great Depression.

A few years ago Alyssa Rae Taylor not only became a bartender at the club, she also became a member. Then, shortly after assuming her duties as the bartender, she started to notice things that weren't quite what most people would call, "normal."

I can hear you muttering right now, "What kind of things?"

Well for instance, one time Alyssa had finished for the night and was clearing the cash register preparatory to counting and reconciling the money with the cash register's tape. The cash cash drawer slid open and she started to take the money out of it.

Suddenly she felt a heavy hand fall on her shoulder. Her heart dropped inside her and, thinking she was about to be robbed, she turned around to confront the person behind her. There was no one there! Just an icy cold presence that slowly faded as she regained her composure. And, over the next few months, it happened twice more.

The bar area only takes up half the first floor. The other half has a dozen or so tables set up in a dining area so that members and guests can enjoy their stay in a more intimate setting. Sometimes that area is the location of entertainment, so there is a small dance area there as well.

More often than she cares to remember, Alyssa has walked through that dining area and looked over the tables and across the dance floor only to see shadow figures projected on the wall behind the dance floor. And this is when there is nobody in the dining area and no lights on that would produce those shadows even if there was somebody there.

As if all that isn't enough, there is the otherworldly activity that takes place on the second floor.

The second floor is mostly one huge open space and is used for wedding receptions, dinners, parties, shows, and the like. When one of these events are scheduled, the floor is cleaned, banquet tables must be set-up with chairs put in place, and so forth. The Lodge's maintenance worker usually takes care of this. So, when Alyssa is at the bar, it is no big thing for her to hear the sounds of those tables and chairs being dragged around, accompanied by the scraping and banging of chairs being put in place.

One afternoon as she was readying the bar for opening, she heard all the commotion of the banquet room being set up. Tables being moved across the floor, chairs scraping along that same floor, and voices of people calling out to one another.

John must've gotten here early to set up, she thought, *Wonder why I didn't hear him come in. Oh well, maybe he just got here extra early to get it done. Funny – nobody told me about any banquet. I guess they're doing their own catering.*

And she went back to her prep work.

Twenty minutes to a half four later, the side door of the Lodge building opened and John walked in.

"Hi John. I never saw you go out," she remarked.

"That's because I just got here," he replied.

"Then who's setting up the banquet room upstairs?"

"Nobody," he replied, "There ain't no banquet tonight."

"But ... but I just heard ..."

The two of them then went upstairs only to find all the tables collapsed and leaned up against one wall, and all the chairs neatly stacked. The lights were off and the room was deserted.

"It's haunted," John told her. "You'll get used to it."

And she did. It happened again again two weeks later.

Other times, when she was the only one in the building, she heard the faint sounds of music and conversation emanating from t he banquet room. She learned to ignore it.

And, finally, out by the Wall of Death, she tried a little experiment. Taking her digital recording device, she attempted to communicate with whatever spirits may be out there.

When she played back her recordings she got two legible EVPs (Electronic Voice Phenomenons).

The first said, "Roster," and she assumed that it referred to the list of members who had passed one.

The second said, "A-R-T, A-R-T, A-R-T." Those are Alyssa's initials and she stopped trying to communicate with anyone on the other side at the Lodge from that day on.

A Ghost's Ghost Story

West Overton Museums

Scottdale

Here's a story of being scared by a spook told by the person who experienced it:

One cold, wet, rainy night in southwestern Pennsylvania, I was getting ready to have a little fun trying scaring some unsuspecting victims at West Overton Museums. I was well aware that the 150 plus year old building and property is haunted by mischievous ghosts. But, I have never seen a ghost nor have been haunted by one, if you don't count the ghost dog and ghost cat that thrive in the attic of the 169 year old house that I call home. Because I have never seen a ghost on this property I figured that he had gone south for the winter. But, since it was around Halloween, just maybe the ghost decided to take a break from the Sunshine State and come up here to spook our little festival.

After I changed into my costume, I went up to the Stock Barn to join my Dad, Mary Ann, Barb, and everyone else. Our job was to read ghost stories to people who came in out of the wind and the rain. My assignment during the readings was to put on my wolf head and wolf-like paws and look scary. I did this job fairly well. Even so, the decision was made to send me up to the hay loft to add to the spooky "atmosphere."

My job changed from standing around looking scary to dragging tow truck chains across the upper floor. When I was up there I had to rough it, so to speak, because I did not have the convenience of light or heat. The only light came from the feeble flashlight that Mary Ann gave me. I used the it to pan around the darkened area. I noticed there was several electric lights hung on the ceiling, but these lights were newly installed and not hooked up to power. I also found up in this loft area a lone galvanized steel garbage can. I decided to beat on that garbage can to try to scare the audience below. I would rattle the chain across the floor and beat the garbage can senseless.

As I made scary noises, I noticed that the wind was

whistling through the holes in the bricks that supported the structure. Like my home, when a big gust of wind hits the building, the floor tends to creak, crack, and make other old building sounds.

As it got close to quitting time, the storm had let up a little, but not enough. We still had one more group to terrify before the night was over. I went back to my post in the dank, dark, cold loft, and resumed my ghostly activities. But there was a little problem this trip. The items in the back of the building were banging rather loudly against the cold ancient brick wall, even though there was no wind whistling through the bricks or the roof rafters. The storm had left the area. Those items banging up against the wall helped me realize I wasn't alone. When the banging stopped, I really wanted to get out of Dodge, and I don't even own a Dodge. Neither does my dad. So, I waited as patiently as I could. I even decided that prayer might help me out, or at least pass the time until I could get to safety. But, this spirit wasn't done with me yet. It decided to walk heavily across the oak wooden floor.

When someone or something walks across a boarded floor, it creaks, cracks, and makes knocking like noises, no matter how well it's installed, or who installed it. As my courage started to evaporate, I made like a TV evangelist begging for God's help. One of the things I was praying for was that Mary Ann would hurry up and finish the story she was reading to her captive audience. As soon as she finished the story and our guests left, I dashed downstairs as though I was being chased by demons. When I got there, I was complemented for my latest performance. Someone told me that I had saved my best for last. I told them that that extra noise was not me. They were convinced the building was haunted and so was I.

The Mystery of the Recharging Batteries

The Geyer Theater

Scottdale, PA

July 19, 2013. A little before midnight in the dark theater. I was a fumbling, inexperienced, neophyte assistant to a psychic who was conducting a paranormal investigation here. I was not completely in the dark, so to speak. I watched enough episodes of various so-called paranormal reality shows on television to know that I was going to need certain things.

First things first, I dressed comfortably. We were at the tail end of a massive heat wave and paranormal investigations are best done with no outside interference from the incessant roar of a commercial air conditioner or four.

I brought my digital camera, a relatively high-end

one that I use for taking pictures to illustrate my books. I also have two crudley-cheapie, low-resolution, digital, throw-away movie cameras that I purchased a while ago just for taking quick movies at amusement parks and when I'm on the road. I brought my digital voice recorder as well, so that maybe I could catch some EVPs. That's "Electronic Voice Phenomenons," to you who aren't as well versed in the jargon of ghost hunting.

Batteries. Lots of spare batteries. That's because spirits need to use a prodigious amount of energy to manifest themselves. They use the smallest amount to talk via digital recorders and then an ever-increasing amount as they appear via orbs, shadows, apparitions on digital camera devices, up to making themselves known audibly to the human ear or visually to the human eye. This energy has to come from somewhere and, for some reason or another, denizens of the spiritual plane have a penchant for getting that energy from batteries, specifically the ones found in cameras, recorders, and flash lights. Being aware of this, I brought plenty of spares for my equipment.

At one point, I was told to set-up a video recorder on the left wing of the balcony nearest the stage, but pointed back to the seats in the center of the balcony. I did this and set it to record, disabling the function that turns it off automatically after a predetermined time.

As soon as it began to record, a white light of undetermined origin appeared on the screen. After about fifteen or twenty minutes of frenzied investigation, we figured out that it originated in the security camera that was trained on the stage. A close examination of the security camera showed no light source whatsoever, but it still showed up on the video as a white light. We attributed it to some sort of electromechanical anomaly that affects the input of my crudley-cheapie video cam in that manner.

We also encountered a red dot on the view screen of the video cam. Much investigation and experimentation showed its physical position to be hovering in the air approximately 1 to 2 feet below, 1 to 2 feet to the right of, and about 6 feet in front of the white light at the location of the security camera. That is, when it stayed still. Eventually, it started moving to the right, then left, up, then down. It waxed and waned in brightness, sometimes flickering. We were unable to determine its origin, energy source, or purpose. It simply existed as a laserlike pin-point of floating energy. We moved on with the investigation, coming back periodically to check the video camera.

We must've gotten sidetracked because nearly 45 minutes elapsed between checks on the camera's operation. During that time, July 19 became July 20, 2013.

Bev noticed it first.

"Ed, the camera has stopped."

"That's impossible." I replied. "I set it so that it couldn't automatically shut off."

"Well, it's off."

"OK, I'll be right there," I grumbled, making the trek across the lobby, up two flights of stairs, down and across the balcony to the camera's location.

The camera was dead. It was off. The screen was blank. So, just to be sure, I pushed the power button. Lo and behold, it turned back on, the battery power indicator showed a full battery, and the timer indicator on the lower left of he screen showed that the timer was turned off. There were only two ways for the camera to shut down: One was for someone to manually push the power button. The other was for the batteries to drain until there was no longer enough power to operate the camera.

Satisfied, I left to pursue other encounters in the realm of spirits. Five whole minutes passed, enough time for me to get as far from the balcony as possible and still remain in the theater.

"Ed?" It was Bev again.

After I indicated that I had heard her, she said, "The camera's off again."

Returning to the camera while bitching, moaning, and complaining, I verified that it was once again, indeed dead (no pun intended.) Pushing on the power button had the same result as before. But this time, I stayed with it to observe. Over a period of less than two minutes, the battery power indicator went from "Full", to "Three-quarters," "One-half," "One-quarter," then "Zero." That "Zero" level was accompanied by a smart-assed, "Good-Bye," on the screen as the camera shut down. I waited maybe thirty seconds and repeated the operation with the same results. Then I went down to the theater lobby, retrieved three new AAA batteries, brought them up to the balcony, and replaced the batteries in the camera with fresh ones.

They lasted less than fifteen minutes and I repeated the procedure with my last three AAA batteries. They also lasted less than fifteen minutes.

Out loud, I said, "Thanks spirits. These were my last AAA batteries."

Down in the open orchestra pit by the stage, Bev distinctly heard a reply, "You're welcome."

Then, I planned an end run on the power-hungry spirit. I'd use my other video cam. When I got it set up and tried to turn it on, all I got on the screen was, "Video card locked," and I was unable to unlock it. All was not lost. There were three unmolested batteries in that video cam! So I swapped them out for the ones in the first cam, with the same results as before. I was treated to a display of a shrinking power bar on the battery level indicator, followed by the aggravating little message, "Good Bye."

Throughout this entire battery-draining episode, I had my Nikon Cool-pix L-310 digital still camera on a neck-strap against my chest for quick access and an Olympus digital voice recorder inside the left breast pocket of my shirt. The batteries in both of these devices were unaffected by whatever was draining the batteries in the video cams.

The Nikon, equipped with four AA-batteries had been on the entire time and, when the evening was over had taken ninety-eight 14-meg pictures with no discernible effect on battery levels.

The Olympus recorded two hours and six continuous minutes, starting at 12:30AM, again with no discernible effect on battery life.

Although I was untrained, for the most part, in paranormal research, I have over twenty years experience in criminal investigations and crime scene preliminary investigations. So, I do know a bit about the scientific method of experimentation and empirical research. Based on this, I came to two possible explanations for the batteries in the video cam draining while the ones in the voice recorder and still camera were not drained.

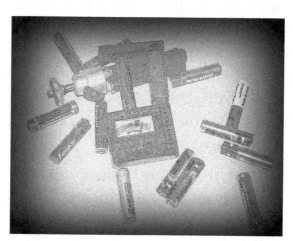

One is that whatever or whoever was responsible for the draining of the camera batteries was localized to that particular spot on the balcony where the video cam was positioned. The second explanation is that, for some reason or another, my personal electromechanical field protected those batteries in close contact with my body from being drained. Fifteen hours after we had temporarily ceased the investigation and returned home, I wondered if I could salvage some of the drained batteries for use in low power situations like clocks. So I hooked them up to my battery power lever meter at home. Each and every one of those "drained" batteries showed a full charge.

All those years of investigation experience, knowledge of scientific methods, and empirical research give me no answer.

ED KELEMEN

The Kecksburg Incident

Kecksburg, PA

No book about unusual events that have taken place in Pennsylvania would be complete without a mention of the Kecksburg Incident.

On December 9, 1965 a fireball streaked across the sky that was observed in six states in the Mid-western United States as well as the Canadian Province of Ontario. Accompanied by a   series of sonic booms, it dropped flaming debris across a 350 mile swath of the United States causing numerous small fires in the process. It lit up the evening sky of Pittsburgh on its way to landfall in the small town of Kecksburg, PA forty-five miles southeast of that city.

Witnesses to the "flash," the "boom," and the ground-shaking "thump," rushed to the place where it landed in the nearby woods. Arriving there, they were confronted by a large acorn-shaped object about the size of a small car with symbols resembling Egyptian hieroglyphics incised along the lower edge.

Shortly thereafter, the military arrived in force, cordoned-off the area, and even evicted local and state police from the site. They blocked all local roads and a heavily-escorted convoy went to the place where the object had landed. Then it was removed from the woods on the back of a flat-bed trailer, completely covered with tarpaulins. The truck was escorted by a convoy of heavily-armed military police vehicles. Then the military completely overhauled the scene and departed, leaving nothing behind.

John Murphy, news director for local radio station WHJB, rushed to the scene arriving before the military and snapped several rolls of pictures of the object. He had planned on using them for a documentary titled *Object in the Woods,* but that was never to be. He was visited by a pair of "Men in Black" who confiscated all photographic evidence that he had been able to obtain, as well as his audio tapes from that evening. A heavily edited version of the documentary was eventually aired with no mention of the object and after some interviewees recanted their statements after being visited by representatives of the government. After that, Mr. Murphy refused to ever talk with anyone about the event. Then, a little over 3 years later, February 1969, Mr. Murphy was struck and killed by a hit-and-run driver while on vacation in California. The case was never solved.

The official explanation for the event was that it was a, "medium sized meteor," that had crashed to earth. No explanation of the "acorn-shaped," or "cone-shaped," object that was seen by witnesses and carted off by the military was ever offered.

In 1996, an opinion was offered that it was debris from a Soviet Kosmos 96 satellite. However, Nicholas L. Johnson, Chief Scientist for Orbital Debris at the NASA Johnston Space Center headquartered in Houston, TX stated, "I can tell you categorically, that there is no way that any debris from Kosmos 96 could have landed in Pennsylvania anywhere around 4:45 p.m. That's an absolute."

Then, eleven years later in 2005, NASA said that it *was* debris from a Russian space satellite. Next, in response to a law suit filed later that same year, NASA stated that they "couldn't find" the boxes of documents related to the incident.

It's a small wonder then, that everyone connected with this incident considered it a prime example of government obfuscation, cover-up, and disinformation.

That's why the Kecksburg Incident is called Pennsylvania's Roswell.

It's memory is kept alive every year during the last weekend in July when the Kecksburg Volunteer Fire Department holds an annual festival in conjunction with the UFO Festival taking place on their grounds.

Sissy's Necklace

Mt. Pleasant, PA

I had been talking with a delightful lady about early marriage and all the trials, tribulations, fun, and complexities of starting off a life together with your loved one. We got on the subject of starter homes and she told me about her first home, saying, "We moved into an old, old house when we first were married. It was about all we could afford, but we didn't know it came with a spirit."

Then she told me her story:

"Today, it would be called a fixer-upper and some

enterprising soul would buy it, repair and repaint it, then sell it for double what they paid. It's called flipping houses. To us, it was just an old run-down house built back in the early 1900s. It was all we could manage and, after paying the mortgage, there wasn't much left over for renovations.

"From that very first day we moved in, I felt uncomfortable there. I always felt as though someone were watching me.

"Then it started.

"A big old hutch that we picked up at a garage sale began to act what I would call weird. Its break front doors opened and closed without warning and without anyone being near it. The drawer that it had would open from time to time and sometimes it would open all the way out. When that happened, its contents spilled all over the floor. And I could never keep anything on it. Anytime I put something on the top, it wouldn't stay up there. I remember putting a bowl with artificial flowers on that top shelf once. It was a nice colorful addition to the room. A few hours later, while watching TV in the living room, I heard the sound of a crash coming from the dining room. I ran to investigate and found that bowl shattered on the floor in front of the hutch, the flowers scattered about. Just to let you know, that old hutch was sturdy, it didn't wiggle or rock, and the floor it sat on was level.

"Later, after our daughter was born, a petty little girl

about 8 years old would appear in the archway between the living room and the dining room. She wore a white shift, patent leather shoes, and a red ribbon in her hair. Like I said before, she was a pretty little thing, but she never smiled. She had the most solemn expression on her face, almost one of a sadness that a child of that age should never have experienced. Other than the experience of a spirit appearing in our home, she was no trouble and we pretty much just accepted her comings and goings.

"Time went by, and Sissy (that's our daughter's nickname), grew into a cute little girl herself who liked all things feminine.

"For her tenth birthday I bought her a nice gold chain necklace with a lapis lazuli stone on it that matched her beautiful blue eyes. It was the first piece of real jewelry that she ever got.

"She had it less than a week when it disappeared. She was heartbroken, blaming herself for not being more careful with it. We turned the house upside-down looking for it. Sissy completely emptied her room and examined everything, one at a time, before returning items to her room.

"Then one evening a few weeks later, our house spirit, the pretty little girl, appeared in the archway again. However, this time something was different. She was smiling for the first time in all the years that she had made appearances in that spot.

"And that wasn't all. She was wearing Sissy's

necklace!

"I was enraged that she had stolen my daughter's necklace.

"And I yelled, "Give back Sissy's necklace! It isn't yours!"

"With that two things happened simultaneously.

"The little girl vanished, never to be seen again. And a wine bottle that had been sitting on the counter in the kitchen flew across the kitchen and into the dining room, smashing itself on the dining room wall next to the hutch.

"And we never again experienced anything supernatural in the house."

I was so taken with her story that I forgot to ask if Sissy ever got her necklace back. I sure hope she did.

The Customer Who Never Left

... Even After He Departed

Mount Pleasant, PA

It isn't all that unusual in the rural parts of Pennsylvania for buildings that formerly housed retail establishments to be converted into homes. This is because those days when people walked to the corner store came to an end. The ready availability of transportation in the form of the family car exploded during the 1950s and marked the beginning of the end of mom and pop general stores.

Then came strip malls and the so-called Big Box stores. They were the final nail in the coffin of small-town general stores.

The area around Mount Pleasant, PA was no different. Each neighborhood had its own general store, and those stores, one by one, went out of business. One of those stores had been in existence since the middle of he 1800s. It was the local place to get groceries, hardware, sewing supplies, and what-have-you. By it's demise in the 1960s, it had served 5 or 6 generations of neighborhood residents.

After lying vacant for a period of time, the building was purchased and converted into a home by the family of the gent who I encountered in Stahlstown, PA in the early fall of 2016. He related the following to me:

At the time, he was about 14 or 15 years of age, he wasn't sure which. It was the early 1960s. He and his mom were visiting relatives who were happily showing off their new digs. Just inside the front door of the store, in the area where all the merchandise had been on display for nearly a dozen decades, was the new occupants' parlor/living room. It wasn't a teenager's idea of a party. All the adults had found their way back to the huge kitchen in the rear of the building where all the food and drink was laid out. Avoiding them, He found himself a nice comfy overstuffed arm chair to sulk in.

After a bit, he became aware that he wasn't alone.

Another person had entered the room. The visitor was a middle-aged gentleman wearing, of all things, a stovepipe hat and a frock coat. It reminded him of the pictures of President Abraham Lincoln he had seen in the history books at school.

Wow, he thought, and continued to watch the fellow. Slightly bent at the neck so as to avoid hitting his hat on things overhead, the gentleman walked about the room looking at things the boy couldn't see. Later on, he figured out that the visitor was looking at items on display in the now long-gone general store.

After watching him for a while, the boy called out, "Hey mister."

And the visitor promptly disappeared, never to be seen again.

Was it a ghost? Possibly a customer from a long time ago looking for someting that wasn't on the shelves during his own lifetime? The gent who told me the story said that he, even to this day, isn't sure exactly *what* he saw, just that he saw *something* or *someone.*

The Wailing Newborn

Norwin Elks Lodge
Manor, PA

The Norwin Elks Lodge sits on 22 beautiful acres in Westmoreland County that was once a farm belonging to a man named Fletcher. Old Fletcher, as he was called by locals, was known for his jams, jellies, and relishes he made on the premises and sold from a barn there. The barn, appropriately enough, was simply called, "Old Fletcher's Barn."

The Fletcher property was purchased by the Elks which instituted the Lodge on December 13, 1964 with an initial membership of a bit over 100. It has prospered and grown to over 750 members today.

Facilities for members include both upper and lower dining rooms, a pavilion that's available to outside groups for rental, a lounge area with two bars and, outside there are even a couple of full-service RV hookups.

Included free of charge, are a few spectres that have taken up residence in the lodge building. They are well known and actually cherished as part of the experience of being a member.

The upper dining room is inhabited by the spirit of youngster who haunts the attic area. From time to time he appears as an out-of-focus apparition who takes his place at one of the unoccupied tables and simply sits there observing the other more mortal occupants of the room. Both diners and employees have encountered him there. There are other unsubstantiated reports of him appearing to and playing with some of the children who live in the nearby neighborhood.

Another haunt of the lodge building is the man who never leaves the bar. Maybe he's waiting for that fabled one "on the house" that he's never going to get. In any case, it's up to the bartender to tell him to leave. And, when he is finally told to leave, he silently walks from the bar, out the door to the parking lot, then vanishes into thin air.

Then there is the basement area of the lodge building. People who have occasion to go there are treated to the sound of incessant dog barking. Trying to find the origin of the aggravating sound is an exercise in futility. There are no dogs there or anywhere else on the property. While trying to locate those dogs, people run into a maintenance man who will dolefully state that the furnace is in dire need of cleaning. If that happens to you, don't bother to answer him. Talking to him just makes him disappear.

Old Fletcher's Barn used to be turned into a walk-through attraction during the Halloween season called the Terror Barn. It was replete with a Michael Meyers Room, torture racks, bloody artifacts, and actors portraying ghosties, ghoulies and psychopaths. What they didn't know was that the barn was already haunted by the spirit of Old Man Fletcher's groundskeeper.

That poor unfortunate was convinced that when Mr. Fletcher sold the property to the Elks he was going to lose his job. Having no other prospects, the depression and despondency that this brought on caused him to commit suicide. He hanged himself in the second floor of the barn near a window. And since he knew no other place he would rather be, his spirit has stayed on, making sporadic appearances in the window that offered him his last view of the outside world while his life slipped away at the end of a rope.

There were a number of other strange occurrences in that barn, but many people attribute them to the props that were used as part of the attraction. The so-called Terror Barn went out of vogue and was closed permanently in 2005.

So far, we've been talking about the better known haunts of the lodge that people have come to accept. In fact, most people feel a sense of being left out if they don't experience at least one of them.

Now, I want to relate to you a lesser-known one that was experienced by a prospective employee of the Elks of Norwin.

>*<

Rhonda Johnston applied for and was offered a job at the Elks as a waitress. Since she personable, attractive, and experienced she was offered the job and given a start date. She showed up on that day and, after a short orientation, went to work.

It was what the other employees described as a typical day, not too slow and not too busy. Her shift went along pleasantly as she learned the ropes of her new position, bustling from table to table exchanging pleasantries with her diners. The busy atmosphere helped the shift pass quickly and, almost before she knew it, the dinner hour was coming to a close and the dining rooms was emptying of diners.

She was off to one side, out of sight of the tables and finishing the checks for the remaining diners when she heard the wailing of a baby coming from the dining room. And she knew that there was nobody out in the dining room who brought a baby with them. Maybe it was someone who had just arrived and had been seated by the hostess. Even so, it wasn't the normal crying of a baby who is announcing that he or she wants a bottle or needs a diaper changed. No, it was more like the heart rending scream of a little one in extreme distress.

It was one of those screams interrupted by that gagging sound an infant makes when it tries to catch its breaths between shrieks.

Rhonda told me that if one of her own children made that sound, she would drop everything and run to the baby to see what was wrong. It raised goose bumps on her arms. So, with her mother's instincts kicking in full bore, she rushed to the seating area of the dining room to offer what assistance she could.

There was nobody there with a baby. The only ones there were those diners still quietly finishing their dinners. She thought that maybe the parents had taken the baby to the rest room or somewhere else to help it out.

So, she went to the hostess and asked her if she had seated any late comers with a baby.

The hostess replied, "No, why?"

"Because I just heard a baby really screaming in the dining room. The little one sounded just awful, as though it was really sick or hurt or someting."

The hostess smiled and said, "Oh, that's just the

ghost of the baby that died. You are very lucky."

Rhonda didn't feel lucky. At the mere mention of the fact that a baby had died and became a ghost, every hair on her body bristled and she was completely covered in goose bumps from an unearthly chill that had taken over her.

"Lucky? How?"

The hostess told her, "Because very few people get to hear the baby cry. You must be special in some way."

Rhonda neither felt lucky nor special. She just felt that she had to leave that place and leave it quickly.

Taking off her apron, she clumped it together, put it on the counter at the hostess' station and said, "I quit."

The hostess said, "Oh no. You don't have to quit, She won't hurt you."

Rhonda repeated, "I quit."

With that she walked out the door, got in her car, and drove away never looking back.

After telling me this story Rhonda told me, "I have never done anything like that, before or since. Something just took over my emotions and told me to get out of there and do it quick."

She also told me that she has never been back to the Elks in Norwin and never plans on going back there.

HAUNTED ANTIQUES

Fort Allen, PA

It was a hot summer day that 4th of July weekend at Twin Lakes Park. I was set up in a quiet wooded lane along with a number of other authors. The afternoon sun had dwindled the crowd, sun dappled the ground under the shade trees, and I was absorbed in watching the dust motes dance in the rays of that sun. All that, combined with a fresh mug of Arnold Palmer-style iced tea meant that I wasn't paying much attention to my surroundings. Another ten seconds and I would have been dozing.

My somnolence was interrupted by a slight cough and I returned to reality with a start. A nice family stood at my table and introduced themselves. They were an elderly couple and a middle-aged son. We talked about this and that for a bit and then the lady asked if I would be interesting in hearing the family's experience with spirits.

Of course you know I said "yes" and this is what she related to me:

"When we were first married, we bought an old house and moved into it as newlyweds. It was one of the first houses ever built in Fort Allen. It was definitely a fixer-upper, but we saw it, not as it was, but as it could be. Besides, we just knew that it would be an ideal location for all the antiques we intended to buy as furnishings and decorations.

"Things progressed nicely and we had great fun restoring the old dowager to her original beauty. After many, many months of scraping, sanding, painting, scrubbing, wiping, digging, and planting, we were finally satisfied with our labor of love. Of course, that didn't mean our work was done. There is always something to do in a building that old.

"Over the years we acquired a plethora of what we like to call "seasoned furnishings." Some people called them antiques and a lot of people just called them junk. Our weekend adventures usually involved digging through stuff at yard sales, garage sales, flea markets, and roadside antique stores.

"The first years of our marriage also blessed us with a son.(Here she introduced him to me).

"But as time went on, we started noticing some strange occurrences in our gem of a home. It started off innocently enough, just the random knock-knock, groan, and creak. We just figured it was the sounds an old house makes, you know just like an old man with arthritis.

"I became concerned when my young son started asking me about the lady in the green dress. At first I blamed it on a youngster's imagination, you know – like having imaginary friends. But he insisted that she was real and she definitely wasn't a playmate. He said that she came and went at odd times, never on any kind of schedule. He saw her in the upstairs hallway and sometimes coming and going from one of the rooms up there.

"A few months later, my husband confessed that he also saw a lady walking around the house and property. His description however, was better. He described her as a young woman of about 30 or so years old, small built, and about five feet tall. She was wearing a white dress with a thingy on her head that he described as a doily. I think he meant that she was wearing a dust cap. He got the impression that she was wearing lace-up boots and she had curly brown hair in the style of a young Shirley Temple.

"He said that he usually saw her in the back part of the first floor where the big kitchen was located and sometimes walking around out back in the garden.

"So far, I hadn't seen anything like the men of the family had seen. Plus, the spirits or whatever they might have been didn't seem dangerous or anything. They just seemed gentle spirits wandering around. I actually thought it was kind of cool to have ghosts in my house. It gave me something to brag about to my less fortunate friends. If only I had known...

"Then it was my turn. One morning I went into the downstairs bathroom. I noticed someting splattered on the wall over the tub. It was brown and looked like it had run a bit. Mumbling something about messy guys, I got some Pine Sol and cleaned it up.

"I mentioned it that evening at dinner. Both my husband and son denied having anything to do with it. Curious.

"The very next day, that splatter was on the wall again. This time, I looked more closely at it and determined that it looked like nothing so much as blood. So I scrubbed it off again and that night chided the men for a not very nice practical joke. Again I was met with denials.

"Well! You can be sure that I checked that bathroom wall first thing the next morning. And – nothing. The day after – again nothing. And every day I checked there was nothing there. I figured that the practical joke had worn thin and they stopped doing it.

"Then one morning two weeks later it was back! I saw the blood-splatter all over the wall just as it had been before. This time, there was going to be no denial. I left it there!

"When my husband and son arrived home for dinner, I escorted them into the downstairs bathroom and said, "Now, just which one of you is responsible for this?"

"They asked in unison, "Responsible for what?"

And the blood spattered wall was perfectly clean. As though it had never been stained. I was baffled."

She went on to explain that she contacted a psychic who did an investigation at her home. The psychic said that she helped the spirits of the two women cross over and that they wouldn't be back. As far as the blood splatter on the wall, she had no idea where it had come from, but suspected that it may be connected to one or another of the spirit ladies. When she asked, the psychic told her that the spirits of the ladies weren't connected with the house, but probably had been attached to one of the antiques she had brought into the house. The psychic advised a cleansing by burning white sage throughout the house, which she did.

And, ever since, there has been no paranormal activity in the house.

She then purchased one of my books for a little girl she knew named Heather. I autographed the book with a short message to Heather, gave it to her, and looked down to make change for the purchase. When I looked up they were gone. Now I had a clear view of at least 100 feet in both directions and could see them neither to the right nor to the left.

Curious.

Babies Crying From the Beyond

Jeanette, PA

Over the years I have refrained from including the old Monsour Hospital in my writings as a haunted location, even though it has been well-known locally as a site of paranormal activity.

"Why so?" you might ask.

Simple, because publicly-accessible places that are known to be hotbeds of paranormal activity draw the attention of those who are less than scientific in their approach to "ghost hunting." Usually young people with nothing to do on an evening who treat it as a lark and leave vandalism, destruction, and empty beer cans in their wake. You need go no farther than to witness the vandalism of graves at Livermore Cemetery by those too unintelligent to realize that it was actually never in the movie, *Night of the Living Dead*. That and the complete destruction of the Amity Hall Hotel in central Pennsylvania by a trio of arsonists trying to smoke out the haunts during a bit of drunken revelry. Then, there is the possibility of youngsters being severely injured in unstable structures. Regardless of how you or I feel about this kind of activity, permanent paralysis or death is not the proper punishment for a bit of youthful indiscretion. After all, we have all been guilty of things that aren't ranked high on our lists of prideful accomplishments.

The Monsour Hospital was never provided with a guard and was only protected by an easily defeated chain link fence. That it was a dangerously unstable structure is demonstrated by the fact that, during demolition of the hospital in February, 2016, an entire section collapsed upon itself and onto the adjacent busy US Route 30 next to it. This east-west arterial highway was completely blocked for hours on multiple days while the debris was cleared.

Now that it is gone, I can offer you the following account of activity there by retired nurse and author of the *Tommy Two Shoes* detective series, as well as a large number of other stories, Tom Beck, who says the following:

"I worked at Monsour for a year before changing hospitals. In the old hospital their surgical intensive care unit was directly above the morgue. I was told that during the night shift, nurses in the unit would often hear babies crying. These nurses were very credible witnesses and I had no reason to doubt what they were saying. I didn't work the night shift often and only rarely worked in the surgical intensive care unit, so I can't confirm what they had heard.

"This hospital was located along a busy four lane highway. The road ran right past the front door of the emergency department. Accident victims were often brought into the emergency room for treatment, no matter how severe the injury.

"It was highly likely that babies and children, as well as adults had died in those accidents and were placed in the morgue until the coroner would release them. At that time there were no air rescue helicopters to fly survivors to trauma units, and some victims would die because that advanced care wasn't readily available.

"The deceased were brought to the hospital as well. The coroners requested that the dead be taken to a hospital to be pronounced by a physician. Most hospitals have stories of ghosts, spirits and of unexplained sightings or sounds."

Any future investigations will need to be done to determine if the spirits have gone the way of the hospital or if they are bound to the grounds of the former healing facility.

ED KELEMEN

The Haunted Television

Latrobe, PA

It is fairly unusual although not unheard of, for a relatively new building to be haunted. Such is the Wyngate by Wyndam located on Route 30 across from the Arnold Palmer Airport in Latrobe, PA. After all, it was only opened for business at the turn of the century in 2000 to take advantage of the rapidly expanding airport.

A former maintenance and cleaning employee told me about a haunted room at the hotel. Actually, it was a haunted television set, one of the new flat screen ones. You see, it had a disconcerting habit of turning itself on and off at random times. Sometimes the guests would be awakened by the roaring volume of the TV which had somehow tuned itself to an action movie. Other times, just at the most important turning point of a movie, sporting event, or show, it would shut off, preventing the guests from knowing how it turned out.

The television set was removed and sent to a repair shop that could find nothing wrong with it. It was replaced in the room and resumed its antics. Only when the TV was removed from the room and replaced with another did the aberrant behavior stop.

When asked, the former employee told me he had no idea what happened to the television set. However, knowing what I do about how hotels dispose of unwanted items, there is someone somewhere in the area who has acquired a "bargain" TV that has a mind of its own. Perhaps an insomniac who doesn't mind loud TV shows in the wee hours.

Caveat emptor, indeed.

The Energy Vampire

Latrobe, PA

During one Halloween Season I happened to give a talk at a library not too far from my home. As usual, my topic was the hauntings and folklore of Pennsylvania. In the audience was a young lady whose pretty and pert appearance caught my eye. And the way she was paying attention to my utterances was quite flattering to this particular septuagenarian.

After the talk I sat at a table autographing books for those who wished to purchase them.

When the meager crowd petered out, she approached me and asked, "Do you believe in vampires?"

"You mean the kind of vampires popularized by Abraham Stoker in the 19th century? If so, the answer is no. Dracula was a pure invention of his imagination, even though he was based on a real person. Vlad Tempe, also called Vlad the Impaler, Vlad Dracul, and Dracula, was a minor warlord who became famous for his penchant of impaling those he considered criminals along the road leading to his stronghold."

I was demonstrating my knowledge of the basis for the fictitious vampire. After all, it isn't often that I get to do so.

She indicated that the blood-sucking, sun-sensitive ghoul wasn't what she had in mind.

So, not wanting to give up the limelight, I continued, "Then do you mean the life-sucking, emotional and spiritual draining kind of vampire? Of course I believe in that type of undead beast. Anyone who has dealt with an ex-spouse's divorce attorney is familiar with that kind of vampire."

No, that wasn't what she meant, although I was getting close.

"I mean the energy vampire," she stated.

I ran down the various energy vampires that I was familiar with. This included all those electronic devices around the average home that are always in what is called "stand-by mode." Some of these, particularly the box that controls home cable or satellite access, can use as much electricity as a refrigerator. I also mentioned desktop computers, printers, and so on.

"No, none of those." And she announced, "I am an energy vampire."

She went on to explain that she was born without the internal cellular structure that allows humans to convert food sources into life-sustaining energy. I'm not sure, but I think she mentioned either a gene or a chromosome that was lacking in her DNA.

She also mentioned that she hasn't a heartbeat and can win bets in a bar by challenging others to find one on her.

Even as an infant she learned how to glean energy from her surroundings. She would drain energy from batteries, electrical devices, and other living beings. For that reason, she was unable to have pets. While merely sitting and petting a kitten or a small dog, she would drain so much energy that the poor animal would expire right then and there.

With other humans, her very touch would drain enough of their life force that they would need to sleep immediately to recoup what she had absorbed.

She had tried to have a normal life, fell in love, and was married. But after a relatively short time, her husband divorced her, even though the two were in love. You see, every time she touched him, he would become extremely exhausted and need to sleep. As time went on, her touch caused him to pass out on the spot as his life force was not being replenished enough between encounters. Fearing for his very life, he divorced her.

She now lives alone with her malady, gaining life force when she brushes against others or "accidentally" bumps into them at places like the mall. That way, she feels that she won't repeatedly drain any one individual. She couldn't live bearing the weight of the guilt that would bring.

Then she announced her intention to leave, saying, "I am sure you understand why I won't shake your hand."

She was right.

Conversation with an Old Friend

Laurel Highlands, PA

Andy had been away from his home town for a spell. Quite a spell. Five years in fact. He wondered how everyone was getting along and whether or not he was finally out of the dog house for a youthful indiscretion. So, he decided to come back for a visit.

Driving down that old tree-lined street brought back an avalanche of memories, both good and bad. He parked his car in front of house number 5010 and walked up the pathway to the porch. Overcome with nostalgia, he pressed the button and was rewarded with the familiar sound of Westminster Chimes from deep within the house.

A few minutes later Andy was at the kitchen table, a steaming mug of coffee at hand, knuckling tears of joy from his eyes. Mom and his sisters acted as though he hadn't ever left, picking up threads of neighborhood gossip that had been dropped all those years ago. He figured he had been forgiven, since nobody mentioned it, and he wasn't about to.

Later that evening he found his way out to the back porch where he had spent so many evenings in the past smoking his final cigarette of the day, while inventorying all that had happened recently.

His reverie was interrupted by a heavy pair of boots landing on the porch floor. Those boots were attached to the feet of his longtime childhood friend and neighbor, Will Henderson.

"Willy, you old so-and-so, it's great to see you!"

Willy engulfed him in a bear hug while stating the obvious, "Andy, it's been years. I missed ya, ya old turd."

The next half hour passed quickly while the long time buddies caught up on things like how the best fishing holes had moved a bit downstream on the Loyalhanna, and how the over-issuance of doe tags had caused a decline in the deer population up Laurel Mountain way. Other things of equal import such as how thrice-divorced Melissa Montague, even after having five children, was still able to attract men were discussed. Andy was shocked to learn that Rolling Rock Beer was no longer brewed in Latrobe, and Willy was amazed that Andy had lost his fear of public speaking and was now giving motivational speeches about that very subject.

Before either one of them knew it, the sun had dropped way below the horizon and the evening had grown chilly. Willy declined Andy's invitation to come inside. Instead, the pair of old buddies parted with an embrace and a hand shake, promising to continue the conversation in the near future.

When Andy went inside, he found Mom watching TV in the living room and told her all about his great visit with his old friend.

As he talked, Mom's expression grew more and more aghast. Concerned, he asked he what was the matter.

And she told him, "Andy, Willy's been dead for two and a half years. He died in a car wreck out on route 30 by the Kingston Dam."

Shadow Beasts
of the Laurel Highlands

Take a ride along any of the two-lane highways that crisscross the Laurel Highlands, especially one of those where the trees form an arboreal tunnel in twilit summer evenings. The best time is as the need for low-beam headlights transposes to the need for high beams.

If you strain a bit, you will be able to see just beyond the fringe of the illuminated area ahead of you.

It is in that nebulous area that the Shadow Beasts dwell.

You can see their movement as something on the edge of your heightened consciousness disappearing around a corner ahead. It's just like that disturbance that occurs at the periphery of your sight when you walk along a deserted hallway.

I have observed the Shadow Beasts myself when traveling along PA Route 711 between PA Route 31 and US Route 30, most often 3 to 4 miles south of Route 30. They have also been seen by kayakers returning from a day on the river along PA Route 381 between Normalville and Ohiopyle, as well. Another place is Route 653 near the top of the mountain where the Laurel Highlands Hiking Trail crosses that road.

What are these Shadow Beasts? I have no idea, and neither does anyone I talked with. The best description that anyone can give is that they resemble stylized cave paintings of animals in motion. They appear to be elongated bison, elk, moose, or bear. And, they always cross the road ahead, just out of your visual focal range.

Is that elongation caused by the stretching of their image as they pass from one dimension to another? I don't know, I just postulate the possibility for argument's sake.

Several times I have stopped my vehicle and searched for evidence of these creatures' crossings, but to no avail. If they have physical properties, they are able to roam without leaving a trace. If they have no physical presence, then ... form your own opinion.

>*<

Shortly after writing the above, I had the following

experience:

In the evening hours of July 20, 2011, a Wednesday, I had another encounter with one of the Shadow Beasts. But this time, I was able to identify the beast.

At 9:30 p.m. it was still swelteringly sticky. The weather this entire week was of the record-setting hazy, hot, and humid variety. Temperatures reached the mid-90s daily.

I took advantage of this by riding my motorcycle to work and rehearsals all week. On Wednesday, after a particularly hot and humid day, I left work in Greensburg and headed for Scottdale some 20 miles south to rehearse for a stage show. Rehearsal ended around 8:45 p. m., just as the sun was disappearing under the horizon. Between work and rehearsal I was pretty well tired out and was looking forward to the ride home through the Laurel Highlands. I welcomed the wind on my face and body and the sudden drop in temperature found in some of the dips and valleys along the way.

It was a nice ride eastward on PA Route 31 and northward on PA Route 711. The miles disappeared under my feet as the evening started to cool off a bit, but not much. The sun started to slide behind the western horizon and the shadows elongated. Finally, all that was left of the summer's sweltering sun was a glow on the western ridges. Route 711 northbound turned into tunnels of verdant green in the valleys.

About three miles north of Route 711's intersection with Route 130, a large, graceful shadow beast bounded across the road. I guess he was startled by my headlight because he paused part-way across the road and turned to look at me with his magnificent antlers silhouetted against the opening at the end of the leafy tunnel. Then he continued across the road and disappeared in the trees and undergrowth.

Shaken, I pulled my bike to the side of the road and stopped to gather my senses. I wracked my brain to identify the huge, beautifully antlered beast I had just encountered. As a hunter, I knew it wasn't one of the indigenous white-tailed deer of Pennsylvania. It was too large and magnificent.

Likewise, it wasn't a stray from the herd of Pennsylvania elk found in the more forested counties of the state. Even with their majestic beauty, they are poor cousins of this magnificent beast. However, I was sure I had seen this animal at least once in the past. Slowly, it dawned on me. It was none other than the fantastic Irish elk, (*Megaloceros giganteous*). I remembered it from many visits to the Carnegie Museum in Pittsburgh when I was a youth.

What makes it problematic is that the Irish elk has been extinct for nearly 11,000 years, and even then it was not indigenous to North America. Its range encompassed Northern Europe, Northern Asia, and Northern Africa.

But, I know what I saw. If the summer twilight filtering through the leaves tricked my eyesight, then the summer twilight did one hell of a job. And did it more than once.

THE LYCAN OF LIGONIER

Ligonier, PA

1905 was a long time ago by any measure. But the elderly gentleman speaking with me had no problem remembering the stories that *his grandfather* told him about life in those times.

He was so descriptive that he made me feel as though I was in Ligonier, PA over 110 years ago. I could savor the mixture of the smell of dust in the air combining with spring flowers and new-mow early hay. Freshly baked bread added to the picture and even the horse droppings weren't offensive, but completed the pastoral scene. The streets and roads hadn't been paved yet, and the gazebo in the town square was still a dream not realized. Even the Lincoln Highway was nearly a dozen years in the future. WWI was a decade away and automobiles were a rarity. Horses and feet provided daily transportation.

As his grandfather told it, their family was a little better off than some. He had a buckboard for transportation and could fit in two other passengers as well as whatever supplies the family needed for the next couple of weeks or so.

At the end of one of these excursions a couple of hours before sunset, because neither the horse nor the buckboard had headlights, it was time to head home. They made their good-byes to their town friends and headed out along the tree-lined dirt road home. Luckily, it hadn't rained lately, so the way wasn't muddy.

They clip-clopped along right smartly, racing the sun. After a bit, the buckboard rounded a curve where the horse came to a stop and refused to proceed another foot forward. The old fellow's grandfather looked up to see what had caused the horse to stop. What he saw made him catch his heart in his throat.

He was faced with the largest, nastiest, most evil-looking canine he ever saw. He couldn't call it a dog because he was sure that no dog ever existed that was as big as the beast that blocked the road that day. It had to be at least twice the size of the biggest dog he had ever encountered or heard about. It was even bigger than any wolf he ever heard about. It was four feet tall to the shoulders. While it presented a formidable and frightening appearance, and even had fangs that extended below its lips, it was the eyes that frightened him. They were without pupils and glowed with a bilious yellow even in the fading daylight. Such malevolence the farmer's son had never encountered in his life. However, he felt a duty to face the animal, if only to protect his fellow family members and his family's horse. He had, after all been entrusted with their care, and he wouldn't even consider letting his parents down.

First he yelled at it. It just continued to bestow upon him that lifeless threatening stare accompanied by a felt, rather than heard, growl. Next, he reached under what today would be called a dashboard, withdrew a couple of pieces of wood kept there for kindling and to use when one or more wheels got stuck. Mustering up all his strength, he heaved those pieces of wood at the animal. He got the same results as before, except that his perception of the unheard growl intensified.

He was loath to escalate the encounter to the next level, but felt he had no choice. He retrieved the rifle from its place under the seat and checked to make sure it was loaded. At ten cents a cartridge, he learned a long time ago to make every shot count. He wasn't afraid to kill the monstrous canine, he was worried about explaining to his father why he spent cartridges on something the family couldn't eat.

Nevertheless, he took careful aim and shot the beast right between those baleful orbs that somehow made himself, his passengers, and his horse so fearful.

Boom! The rifle's sound filled the air along that

country lane. The bullet flew straight and true into its target. And...

...Nothing! The creature didn't even flinch. The young fellow figured that his days had just come to an end there and then. He started to make his peace with The Lord before sacrificing himself to save the others. He alighted from the buckboard and approached the creature. He wasn't sure what to do, but he figured he had to do something. When he got about 15 feet from the thing, it shook its head from side to side, turned, and calmly walked into the trees lining the road and disappeared. It was seen from time-to-time by others in the area, but never again by his grandfather.

>*<

UPDATE

This sighting has a modern connection. In roughly the same area that the canid creature was spotted in 1905, it was spotted again in 2008. John MacDonald, a member of the Center for Cryptozoological Studies made the following report about a sighting of a similar creature in Ligonier:

"The Ligonier Lycan"
Date: August/Early September 2008
Time: 10:00 PM

Two eyewitnesses were outside on the porch with their adult son having a smoke and enjoying the warm night. They had the flood lights on watching deer feed in the grassy area above them. The deer spooked and ran across the hill in the same direction they always go, from what the witness said.

Suddenly, a dog-like creature running on all fours sprinted past them about 20-25 feet away from the porch on the upper grassy embankment, possibly chasing the deer on the hill. Both witnesses said as it ran past it glanced at them. They think it might have been surprised that they were there. The eyewitness said the eyes were yellow and the fur was coarse and dark or gray. It had a long snout and a "powerful torso". They estimated the size to be about 48 inches from the shoulder to the ground. When it ran the motion reminded her of a greyhound in a full deep strut. The eyewitness states that both legs were stretched out and were in sync when it ran. It was relatively quiet as it briefly passed them. There were no smells associated with the creature. The witnesses had large dogs as pets before and it exhibited similar dog-like traits, however they both agreed it wasn't a dog that they saw.

Is it the same animal making sporadic appearances for over a century? Or is it descendants of that animal? And where does it go between sightings?

These are all questions the members of the Center for Cryptozoological Studies are striving to answer.

THE HEADLESS CHILD

Ligonier, PA

Another story related by the gentleman's grandfather was about the headless child.

As people traversed the lanes, roads, and paths of the turn of the twentieth century Ligonier, PA area, another unsettling apparition caused them consternation.

At random times of the day, at random locations, a small child walked slowly out of the trees and stood in the middle of the road. It was always assumed that the child was a girl of about eight because she was wearing a sackcloth dress and was about the right stature for a girl of that age. These assumptions were necessary because the little one had no head. Her body ended at her neck.

The little girl never made any threatening movements, she just stood silently in the middle of the road. After the initial shock, folks grew used to her appearing here and there, so they simply steered their horses around the apparition and proceeded on their way. That is, until one day when a boy of about 12 was heading home from town with his younger brother along. They had completed a list of errands for their parents and were enjoying the ride in a single horse drawn trap. A trap is a 2-wheeled cart with a seat for two. Right under and behind the seat is a wooden trunk for storage. It was the sports car of the day.

They were moving along at a quick trot enjoying the wind on their faces when the little girl suddenly walked out onto the road. For whatever reason, the horse reared up and turned sharply, overturning the trap and spilling both boys onto the ground.

The older boy felt a sharp pain in his right arm. Later examination revealed the arm to be broken. The little girl vanished and was never seen again. Perhaps, not meaning to cause hurt to anyone, she may have felt guilty about the lad's injury.

In any case, she never returned.

The Mirror

Near Ligonier, PA

A middle-aged gentleman, obviously in great health and physical condition, along with his wife who was also obviously partakes of the healthy lifestyle bought both of my books about the hauntings along Pennsylvania roadways: *Pennsylvania's Haunted Route 30* and *Pennsylvania's Haunted Route 22*.

Thumbing through the book about Route 30, he commented, "I see you missed one."'

That piqued my interest, so I asked' "How so?"

Here's what he told me -

Right off Route 30 in the Ligonier area was a house that dated all the way back to the 1830s. It was in such a deteriorated condition that it couldn't be restored and was scheduled for demolition.

On a particularly sweltering August afternoon he noticed the workmen preparing the site, so he asked the supervisor wearing the white hard hat if he could look around.

"No skin off my nose," was the reply. He took this as tacit permission, so he and his wife went on in.

They were amazed to find a lot of the contents still in place. But most of them were just old, not antique, and in such a state of disrepair as to be only fit for kindling wood. It looked like squatters had been living in the house for some time. But the intrepid pair of "diggers" persevered, examining all the nooks and crannies they could find. Eventually that doggedness paid off when a closet yielded treasure.

Treasure to them, that is. To anybody else it was just a filigreed and gilded old mirror showing the patina of age. And dust, lots of dust.

"Honey, this mirror would be perfect for over the table in our foyer," she exclaimed.

He agreed. It fit the style of that old table and was the perfect size as well.

Sneezing in the cloud he created by blowing the dust layer from some of the filigreed decorations., he commented, "It'll go perfectly with that statue of Dad's that we put on that table."

Right here I interrupted his story to ask why he had

a statue of his dad in the foyer.

He explained that it was a statue that had previously *belonged* to his dad, not a statue *of* his dad. That point cleared up, he continued.

He picked the mirror up and removed it from the closet. Suddenly the temperature dropped enough to give both of them a chill.

"Honey, let's get out of here," his wife demanded.

The old house was then filled with the sounds of doors and windows slamming shut.

He grabbed the mirror and they headed for the door which was now closed. They had to struggle with it to open it.

"Looks like the mirror doesn't want to leave its home," he quipped.

But they took the mirror away anyway, cleaned it, and gave it its place of honor in the foyer. But it brought with it a sense of foreboding and suspense. It looked great, but it made them uneasy whenever they looked into it.

"It's kind of hard to explain," he said. "It was always as though an unseen someone was looking over my shoulder when I looked into it, An unseen someone who bore me ill will. And I wasn't the only one who felt that way."

They decided that, even though the mirror fit so well into the foyer decor, it had to go. They decided to only keep it until they could find a replacement.

The mirror must have sensed their intentions because one day it "fell" from its place on the wall. As it fell, it struck the statue, cleaving the head from it as neatly as a guillotine. But the mirror survived the "fall" without damage, not even scuffing the gilt.

They waited no longer and got rid of it immediately by donating it to a church based resale shop where, they hoped, its anger would be dissuaded.

>*<

I hope that you, dear reader, haven't purchased it at a church rummage sale.

One Opinionated Grandmother

Loyalhanna Gorge

Ligonier, PA

A lady told me this story while I was doing a book signing outdoors in the middle of a thunderstorm:

"My grandmother was always a feisty lady, what with being the matriarch of the family and all. It was a great loss to the family when she passed away during 1981. But the pain of her passing was slightly alleviated by the birth of my niece, who was named after her.

"As time went on, my niece not only resembled Gram physically, as we could tell from early pictures of Gram; she had Gram's personality as well.

"Everyone in the family constantly commented on how much Elizabeth was just like Gram. I'm sure that it must have irritated her to be always compared to someone she never met and never would meet. We even called her Little Elizabeth to differentiate her from Gram, who some people called Big Elizabeth.

"One day I was driving along Route 30 with my sister in the car and we were talking about our Little Elizabeth and her mannerisms, appearance and so on.

"As we were passing the little dam at Sleepy Hollow where cars constantly have to be rescued when they try to go across when there is water flowing over it, my sister, said, "Why, I believe that Little Elizabeth is the living reincarnation of Gram."

"The inside of the car grew icy cold like when a window is open in the winter and Grandmother's unmistakable voice came from the back seat.

She said, clear as day, "No she isn't!""

To hear this story punctuated by thunderclaps was enough to make the hair on the back of *my* neck stand on end.

SPIRITS FROM THE
LITTLE CHURCH ON THE HILL

Fairfield Township, PA

Later on is a story about a fellow who got an incredible deal on a load of concrete blocks, only to find that they had come from a cursed building built over a Native American burial ground. His experience with those bargain basement-priced building materials wasn't a good one. Likewise the couple who "discovered" an antique mirror in an abandoned house scheduled for demolition earlier in this book.

People never seem to benefit from the experience of others when it comes to the perception of saving a few dollars.

Case in point:

A few years back, a local church in Fairfield Township, about fifteen miles north of Ligonier, had gone defunct for one reason or another. The red-painted old wooden house of worship, and its adjoining cemetery came on the market for an astonishing low price. That alone should have raised a warning flag. But, not to a family in need of both building materials and land. It was ideal for their purposes.

One member of the family was in desperate need of wood to construct a two story addition on his cramped home. Another found that the spot where the church building sat was an ideal location for a mobile home, even though the back yard was full of graves.

No problem. Family members pitched in as they are wont to do in rural Pennsylvania where family ties are strong. In no time at all, the church building was reduced to a few orderly piles of lumber with the nails removed, all ready for its next incarnation. The land where the venerable building had sat was cleared, graded, and made ready for the mobile home.

And then the construction began in earnest.

The mobile home was set up in less than a month and shortly thereafter children brought their own brand of happiness to the place as they played and shouted with youthful enthusiasm.

While this was being accomplished, the other brother, let's call him Mike, commenced to build that addition on the small cabin that he, his wife, two daughters, and a baby son called home. It was framed with ancient timbers, roofed with slate, and floored with some of the best hardwood that grew on the aptly-named Chestnut Ridge. Finally, the family of five could stretch out in a home worthy of their numbers. And everybody had their very own room!

And so it went. For the next few months everyone was happy in their new digs. Then things began to happen. Strange sounds at night, things moving on their own, phantom footsteps.

The ones in the house most affected by the otherworldly events were his two daughters. And they tried to tell Mike about those strange things that were happening in their home.

Mike refused to acknowledge the strangeness of the events taking pace in his home. You see, he was a no-nonsense kind of guy who believed that there is always a rational explanation for everything that happens.

The noises at night were nothing more than the regular noises of new construction settling. The reason they are heard at night is because the sounds of daylight traffic on the road, people talking, and the television drown them out during the day. Nothing moves on its own, people just imagine it. Same with the footsteps, they are the product of overactive imaginations.

Then, one day the girls started communicating with

whatever or whomever was making the noises, only this time it was during the day. You see, there sounded a series of knocks from inside the wall of the newly-constructed addition.

The older girl, we'll call her Melanie, got what she thought was a good idea.

She said to her younger sister, "I know how we can talk with the ghost that's making all the noises. We can talk with it with the knocks on the wall. We can use one knock for yes and two knocks for no."

Using this method of communication, they were able to find out that the knocking in the wall was being done by a young girl who had died and was buried in the little cemetery by the now demolished church. They learned the little one's name by going through the alphabet one letter at a time. It was Sarah, and she became a secret friend of theirs.

Melanie asked Sarah if she wanted something. The answer was one knock.

"What is it?" she asked. Two knocks was the reply.

"That means it's too complicated to tell us with knocks," Melanie told her little sister, Kat.

"What can we do, then," she asked.

There was one knock as an answer. But this knock was farther along the wall. So the two girls went to that location. There came a knock a few feet farther along the wall.

"Do you want us to follow you?"

One knock, which was followed by another knock farther along the wall.

In this manner the spirit led the two girls out of their room, along the wall, down the steps to the lower floor and eventually ended up at a point in the downstairs hall where the knocks went no further.

"What do you want us to do?"

Three knocks on the wall.

"Is there someting here?"

One Knock.

"Is it behind the paneling?"

One knock,

"Do you want us to get it for you?"

One knock.

"Is it right here?"

A whole series of excited knocks.

These two youngsters were their father's daughters. They knew more about home construction that the average adult, let alone kids. They could hammer nails without damaging wood and could repair drywall without leaving a trace. So, it was no problem for them to carefully remove a section of wall paneling. All it took was a nail remover and some judicious maneuvering.

At first they were disappointed because they saw

noting behind the panel. Kat ran and got a flashlight and shone it into the space behind the panel. They saw something wedged back up against a 2×4. Kat was the skinniest, so she wriggled her way in a bit, stretched out her arm and withdrew the item.

Again, they were disappointed. It was just an old arm broken off a baby doll.

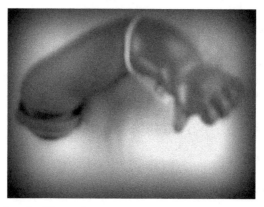

Melanie asked, "Sarah, is this what you wanted us to find?"

One knock.

"Is it yours?"

One knock.

"How did it get inside the wall?"

Three knocks, which, by now, they figured meant, "I don't know."

Kat interrupted the conversation by saying, "We better get that panel back in place before Dad gets home. We can talk with Sarah later."

And that's what they did. When they were finished, the panel and the trim was back in place looking like it had never been disturbed.

That night, when the girls settled in their beds, a tentative knock came from the wall.

Kat answered first this time, "Oh Hi Sarah, do you want to talk?"

One knock.

"What do you want us to do with your baby doll's arm?"

Using their private code of knocks, Sarah eventually made known to Kat that she wanted her baby doll's arm back with her.

So, the following weekend, Kat and Melanie hopped on their bicycles and headed to their uncle's place where Sarah's grave was located behind his family's mobile home.

They got down on their knees and, using an old garden trowel, dug as deeply as they could into Sarah's grave. When they figured that the hole was deep enough, they placed the baby doll's arm into it, filled the hole back up, and said a few prayers before heading back to their home.

That evening when the girls were upstairs, a knock came from inside the wall again. It was Sarah. She came back to say thank-you and good-bye.

The girls were happy that they were able to help

and they never heard from Sarah again.

The rest of the restless spirits weren't as easily satisfied as Sarah. The sisters weren't able to communicate with them and so the barely-heard whispered conversations that Melanie and Kat just couldn't quite understand continued. Whomever liked to clomp up and down the steps kept right on doing it, and small items still tended to fall off shelves and sometimes fly across rooms when nobody was in those rooms. And their dad, Mike, still opined that all the things that happened like that was because the house continued to settle.

The house was still "settling" on its foundation when Melanie got married and moved out years later. It continued to "settle on its foundation" when Kat moved out a couple of years after Melanie.

The uncle, aunt, and covey of children who lived in the mobile home where the old church originally stood weren't as practical as Mike. Except Mike's sister-in-law, Emma, preferred the term thick-headed. Emma, Noah, and their kids were believers.

In the evening hours they saw with their own eyes the shadowy shapes flitting from grave to grave in the little cemetery that was their back yard. Sometimes on a Sunday morning they heard faint strains of piano music and hymns sung by a church choir being carried on the morning breeze. Footsteps in the home's hallway, cabinets opening and closing on their own, and little objects being moved about were just part of daily life.

As Emma says, "We have taken up residence in their home, not the other way round. Besides, we kinda like them. We feel that, just as we are watching over their graves and tending to them, they are watching over and protecting us."

For you who are reading this – just remember that bargain building materials ofttimes come with more than the materials alone.

A Hungry Ghost?

New Florence, PA

This tale goes back generations and was told to me by an octogenarian who said that her mother told her the story. Furthermore, it was at a meeting of church ladies, so I just *know* that it must be true. Here's what she had to say:

"Back in my childhood days, we children liked to roam all over the hills and valleys around our little rural town. It was back in the day when we had a hotel and train station right in town next to the feed mill. The bridge across the Conemaugh was about a quarter mile downstream from where the new bridge is now. The old bridge got washed away in the big flood.

"Anyhow, there's this big old hill that overlooks the valley a little ways south of town. It's called Squirrel Hill. I don't know why, I never saw any squirrels up there, just lots of rabbits. Now, somewheres or another up there, an Indian chief is rumored to have died. How he died isn't really known, but most people said that he starved to death during a nasty winter.

"Like I said, as children we liked to roam all over that place. It was a good berry-picking place and we liked to go up there, have a little campfire, and spend the night from time-to-time.

"Well, it never happened to me, but my mother says it happened to her brother a long time ago. You see, if you sleep on that hill all night and get up in the morning and start to cook over the campfire, you will hear the old Indian chief moaning like he was in pain or something.

You won't see anything, but you can hear him clear as a bell. After a while, if you ask him what he wants, he will say, "Breakfast." And if you throw a bit of what you are cooking into the underbrush, he will stop moaning and leave you alone."

I assured her that I would never venture up on Squirrel Hill without an extra Egg Muffin for the hungry Indian chief.

A Quirky Little Haunt

New Florence, PA

I'm not sure when it started, just when I noticed it. It's kind of like the sock-eating washer-dryer thief in the laundry room. Except when a sock disappears, it never comes back.

For a while I just chalked it up to that famous guy: Coincidence. After all, it was just small things that could easily fall to the floor and roll out of sight. Things like keys, pens, pencils, combs, eyeglasses, and so forth. A prescription bottle of pills. A computer flash drive.

When you live in a grand old house with a trio of big dogs and a clutch of attitude-ridden cats, you learn that things sometimes disappear. Often into omnivorous gullets. I didn't know that there might be another explanation. Until it was forced on me.

Then, and only then, did the realization that we were sharing our home with yet another otherworldly presence slowly sink in. How was I made aware of the presence? When missing things came back to places they didn't belong.

The first was a tape measure. Not just any tape measure, but one that measured distances up to twenty-five feet. It weighs about a pound and is a handful. One day I needed to measure something in my office, what it was is of no consequence. I made the necessary measurement and placed the tape measure on my desk while I wrote the measurement down on a pad. When I turned back to the desk, the tape measure was gone. I searched that room high and low with no results. I even looked under tables, chairs, and cabinets. I checked the window sills, along with every other flat surface in that room, all to no avail. I went and got another tape to finish the measurements that I needed to get. I tried to forget about the first one figuring that one of the dogs now had a new plaything.

Three days later the tape reappeared dead smack in the middle of a newly-made bed in my office, a spot that is constantly under my observation when I am working at the computer.

That's odd, I thought and asked everyone else in the house if they had put it there. Nobody had.

Next, my wife lost her glasses necessitating a trip to the eyeglass store to have her old pair repaired to the point where she could use them temporarily. They came back to us by appearing on the kitchen counter, which was bare of everything but those glasses. Again, a couple of days had passed.

My son set down an electric drill while working in the basement, only to have it enter another dimension for a while until it reentered our reality two floors up and two days later.

A young friend of ours was using one of our portable telephones when she dropped it. It hit the floor and the battery cover detached and skittered across the floor and under a chair. I knelt down to recover it, only to find that it wasn't there.

"That's it!" I shouted, "I've had it. You better bring back my battery cover and bring it back now!"

Of course there was no answer. But, when I went into then kitchen fifteen minutes later, the missing battery cover was lying on the kitchen table.

The last straw came the day that I was putting a framed award up on the "I Love Me Wall" in my office. I was using that same big, bright yellow tape measure that had previously disappeared from that self-same office.

I was treated to a repeat performance. I made the necessary measurement, just as before. I placed the tape measure on my desk, just as before. I wrote the measurement on a pad, just as before. I reached for the tape to verify the measurement, just as before. And it was gone, just as before.

I must confess that, at that point, I lost it. I went into a profane tirade the gist of which was that, if I didn't get my tape measure back, and get it back soon; there was going to be an exorcism in my house.

A few minutes later, I went to the kitchen to brew a cup of coffee while I settled down.

The tape measure was lying in a place of prominence on the kitchen counter near the coffee maker.

"OK, you slide this time. Don't let it happen again," I informed the wayward spirit.

Of course, he or she paid me no mind and these incidents just increased.

I admit it is a minor irritation, but we have actually welcomed this somewhat mischievous, but harmless spirit into our whacky family. So far, he or she hasn't taken anything of consequence and everything has been returned within a couple of days to a place where it is easily noticed. And I now own at least 4 tape measures. Just in case.

And, it can serve as a companion to our other ghostly presence, Brownie, the ghost dog.

Oh, you don't know about our ghost dog? Well then, just read on, it's the next story.

Our Spectral Canine House Guest

New Florence

New Florence is a small bucolic town nestled in a valley of the Laurel Highlands. Its most notable feature is its tree-lined streets festooned with blossoms in the spring, leaves in the summer, riotous color in the fall, and snow in the winter. It's a place where everybody knows everybody and most doors are left unlocked. Those are the reasons that we moved here some twenty-five years ago.

We bought a stately old dowager of a frame house that had seen well over a hundred summers and winters. It sits on a corner lot across the street from a church and sleepily watches over the intersection. We fell in love with it at once and hurriedly moved in. Shortly thereafter, our two young sons started complaining about noises in the attic. We told them not to worry; it was probably mice that our cat, Velvet, would make into a dinner for himself..

One evening my wife asked, "Why is Satin (our female black lab at the time), running around upstairs?"

I replied that I'd check, and went to the second floor to see what was causing the ruckus. When I was half-way up the stairs, I noticed Satin sitting at the bottom of the stairs wagging her tail. I got to the top of the stairs and rounded on the hallway just in time to see the southern half of a medium-sized shaggy brown dog enter one of the front bedrooms. I rushed into the room, only to find it empty.

This started a series of sightings of the shaggy brown dog, mostly on the second floor and on the stairways. For some reason, we have gotten the impression that the dog is a male and we have named him Brownie. None of us has seen the entire dog at once. What we have observed is him entering or leaving a room. We have seen his backside disappearing into a room, or his face and head poking around a corner of a doorway. Sometimes, all that can be seen is his brown paws extending from a room. The boys have heard a continuation of the sound of dog nails clicking on the floor of the attic.

Rather than a menacing or baleful impression, we get a feeling of comfort when we know Brownie is about. We told the boys that we have an extra canine presence helping to guard the home. That satisfied them.

Over the years we have accumulated more pets and currently have two humongous dogs, as well as a clutch of cats. The dogs have accepted the presence of their spirit equivalent with equanimity, reacting to his presence with nothing more than a cocked ear or a quizzical expression.

The cats, on the other hand, are fascinated, and seem to be able to notice Brownie's presence even when he isn't visible to us. Frequently two or more of the cats will sit together swiveling their heads in unison while apparently following the progress of the dog up and down the stairway, or across the room. They also attempt to interact with him on the second floor landing, trying to pat him with their paws and get a game of,"Catch me if you can," going.

A nylon bone left on the second floor for Brownie to gnaw on has often been moved from where it was left. It is just as likely that one of the cats or our other, more corporeal dogs has moved it as it is that our spiritual canine has played with it.

And, now, after all these years, we accept our canine specter as one of the family and even call out to him to watch the home while we are away.

We say, "Hey Brownie, watch the house. And, if anyone comes in while we're away, scare their pants off."

An Encounter With Big Bird

West Wheatfield Township, PA

On Wednesday, October 1, 2014 at approximately 4:15PM, I was on my way home from Blairsville, PA. I live in the small town of New Florence in the Conemaugh Valley just upstream from Packsaddle Gap. Although it is only about 6 miles from Blairsville by way of the railroad, it is nearly 20 miles by road. That's because the only road access from that direction is by going over the Chestnut Ridge on Longview Mountain via US Route 22, then south on Pa Route 259 to Mulligan Hill Road, then up and over Mulligan Hill. The top of Mulligan Hill is plateau-like and planted with corn on the west side of the road. To the east of the road, the hillside falls away. Then the road drops about 200 feet over a space of 1/4 mile through a wooded area to the bottom. The location is about 2 miles in a straight line from the New Florence Electrical Generating Station and about 6 miles from the Seward Electrical Generation Station.

OK, the preceding is just background to give you an idea of location and place. Both the wooded area and the cornfields at the top of the hill are heavily populated with wild turkeys. Many times, while driving along this stretch of road, I have been startled by a wild turkey flying over my vehicle from one side of the road to another. I tell you this to let you know that I can easily identify a wild turkey in flight.

On this particular afternoon, the weather was clear and warm with a temperature in the mid 70s.

As I was driving down the slope heading south on Mulligan Hill Road, a large black shape flew over my vehicle nearly blotting out the sunlight. It was much larger than the largest wild turkey I'd ever seen. I cannot begin to identify the creature, I can only describe it.

It was either black or extremely dark brown with an elongated neck similar to a goose or a heron and flew in a rising trajectory from east to west over the road. I think that its beak, which resembled that of a raptor was a light brown, but I'm not 100% sure. Its legs, which were tucked up into its body and trailing behind had talons and were also a light brown. The bird, if that's what it was, had an approximate wingspan of 12 feet and it was about 12 to 15 feet in length. It was completely covered in feathers and the trailing edge of the wings had feathers extending behind it, similar to the flaps on an airplane wing. Also, it may have been flying soundlessly, because I could not hear it over the sound of my car's engine and tires.

And, it flew from the tree line to the left into the tree line to the right of my car, keeping in mind that the density of the tree line is such that a bird of this size could not possibly have fit between those trees. My only explanation is that it flew from one plane of existence to the left of the road into my plane of existence as I traveled the road and then into yet a third plane of existence to the right of the road. That's what it did, I have no explanation of how it accomplished the feat.

You may wonder how I was able to gather so much information and description in the short amount of time that it took to glide over my car. I can offer two reasons. One, it imprinted itself on my memory since it was such an unusual event. Two, the damn thing was no more than 15 feet above my car! I'm just glad that it was holding its bowels or it would have broken a window at the very least.

The Book Burning Spirit

Johnstown, PA

Elsewhere in this book is a list of other books I have written, mostly in the field of paranormal events such as hauntings. One of these books is titled *Pennsylvania's Haunted Route 22.* It is for sale at a number of places along that venerable highway that extends the whole length of the state.

As far as I know, people who have read the book thoroughly enjoy the trip along this haunted highway that they can take without ever leaving the comfort of home.

One of the places that *Pennsylvania's Haunted Route 22* is available is at *The Bottle Works Arts on 3rd Avenue* Gallery Gift Shop in Johnstown, PA. I made arrangements for this with the able assistance of Todd Stiffler, the Assistant Director of the gallery. Part of our arrangement was that I would periodically check in to make sure that my display was adequately stocked with books.

One day in July, 2016 I stopped in and checked the display. I saw two copies of *Pennsylvania's Haunted Route 22* were missing from the shelf so I did my happy dance. It meant I had made some sales and could eat for another month!

While I freshened up the display, Todd came out of his office and greeted me with, "Something weird is going on with your books."

"How so?" I responded.

"It's easier to show you than to tell you," he replied and continued, "Follow me back to the storeroom."

When we got there, he rummaged on a shelf and withdrew the two supposedly sold copies of *Haunted Route 22*. He handed them to me, saying, "Look at the edge of the pages."

I did. The edges of the pages opposite the spines exhibited a burn mark 2-12 inches long and totally across the thickness of one copy of the book and about half-way across the thickness of the other copy.

"Damn." It was the extent of my vocabulary at the time.

I examined the books. The char mark was mostly on the long edge of the pages, it extended less than 1/2" across the top. Nothing else on the shelves had been disturbed in any way. There was a display of candles on the shelf below, but none had been lighted.

So, my first impression was that someone had held the two books together in one hand while applying the flame of a pocket lighter or candle to the outside edge of the books. But a sniff test indicated that the charring was not as a result of a flame being applied to the book. It had none of that burn odor that paper gets when burned. Sniffing also ruled out a chemical burn as the culprit.

An examination of the windows nearby that allowed sunlight to enter the gallery revealed nothing that could possibly have been used as a lens, so that was eliminated as well.

The only other explanation was an otherworldly one. Possibly there was a spirit nearby that, for some reason or other, didn't care for the stories of haunts in the book.

"Everyone's a critic," I commented to Todd. I took the books away for further examination.

>*<

Lady Luck smiled on me and I had occasion to meet

with the Psychic Vincent Sisters of Pittsburgh a few days later. They are a pair of well-known and well-respected psychics who have been involved in the solution of countless cases of missing persons and murders. They are frequently called on by various law enforcement agencies when those agencies meet a dead end in their own investigations.

So, I asked them their opinion of what may have happened with the books.

When Suzanne Vincent clasped the books between her hands, she said, "There is a very angry spirit attached to these books. I will attempt to contact him and try to determine what is his problem."

After a bit, she went on, " In his former life the spirit was a college professor of psychology. He says that books ruined his life and he just took his anger out on these two books. He has nothing specific against you, (meaning me) and is sorry if he caused you (meaning me) any inconvenience."

She then privately conversed with him for a while to see if she could possibly bring him to terms with what had happened in his mortal life that caused his anger and hatred.

"He is glad that his anger didn't cause any more damage than it did and promises to never try to harm anyone or anything at the gallery again."

With that, she handed the books back to me and told me not to worry, it was a one-time thing and won't be repeated.

A couple of days later, I met with Beverly LaGorga, co-author of her biography, *We Don't Talk About Those Kind of Things – The Making of a Psychic,* and asked for her opinion of how the burn marks came to be on the books. Just as I did with he Vincent Sisters, I gave her absolutely no background information on the books as I handed them to her.

Beverly's response was identical to Suzanne's, also assuring me that it won't happen again.

As for me, I'm happy to see this resolved.

>*<

Todd was relieved when I returned to the Bottle Works and informed him that there would be no future spiritual book burning taking place on the premises.

Domestic Relations Don't Necessarily Ensure Domestic Tranquility

Ebensburg, PA

If you take a ride along Manor Drive in Ebensburg, PA you will be rewarded with some of Pennsylvania's most beautiful scenery along the winding road through the rolling countryside. As you travel along, watch the right side of the road. At 499 Manor Drive you will see a complex of buildings on that side. The rectangular three story red brick building is the home of Cambria County's DRC, or Day Reporting Center.

The Day Reporting Center program is one that is designed to help alleviate recidivism within the county's criminal justice system and to more smoothly reintegrate convicted offenders back into society. Persons allowed into the DRC program are required to report every day, in person, to complete a three-level treatment program that is specifically designed for each client. Not only does the program teach the clients life skills and understanding that allows them to become productive members of society, it also costs quite a bit less per client to the taxpayer than incarceration.

The DRC program was started in May, 2013 and shows great results in rehabilitation. After a bit of shuffling here and there, it settled in the ground floor of that old red brick building which is also the home of the Cambria County Domestic Relations Office.

The Domestic Relations Office is responsible for, "all matters establishing the paternity for children born outside of marriage and in establishing and enforcing financial and medical support for minor children and, if appropriate, dependent spouses." Their words, not mine.

OK, what does all this have to do with anything?

Well, a friend of mine got caught up in the slow moving, grinding wheels of justice a while ago. After serving 90 days in the county lockup, he was admitted into the DRC program which meant that he had to report and take classes six days a week as he moved up through the three levels of treatment.

He usually had a bit of time on his hands while waiting for the public bus service to make its stop at the DRC for the hour-long trip back to Johnstown some 25 or so miles away. During this time, he made the acquaintance of a number of the maintenance workers at the facility. After a while, when he had gained their confidence, they began to tell him stories about that old red brick building.

The evening cleaning crew has had some experiences in there that don't quite fall under everyday happenings.

One day, the conversation turned to these occurrences. It went like this:

"Did you know that this building is haunted?" One of the workers asked him.

"No way!" he replied.

"Yes way. I've heard things myself," the worker came back with. "Things like heavy footsteps clomping along the hallway upstairs where the Domestic Relations Offices are."

"Yeah," another of the maintenance staff chimed in, " And what about those arguments and fights that take place up there all the time at night when there is supposed to be nobody there?"

"We are supposed to be the only ones in the building after hours," the first worker said. And he went on, "But sometimes it sounds like there's a bunch a people running around, arguin' and fightin' up there."

"And, when we first heard it, we used to run up there to see what was going on. And there would be nobody there."

The second guy added, " What about all the times we go up there and someone, or something turns off the lights?"

"Right you are," the first worker came back. "And how many times have we heard the radio playing up there only to have it turn itself off when we enter the hallway?"

The two workers then snubbed out their cigarettes, patted my friend on the back and took his leave, telling him that they'd see him again the next day.

Is the building haunted? Maybe, but not by spirits. If it's haunted by anything, it's by the raw and intense emotions that are played out at Domestic Relations on a daily basis. Emotions that are so bitter, vehement, and harsh that they get imprinted into the very building itself, only to be played back when calmness and quietude settles in the velvety darkness of the night. Velvety darkness that insures that anybody who encounters them will be spooked.

The Haunted Paper Mill Bridge

Roaring Spring, PA

Morrison's Cove is a natural declivity in the mountainous area just south of Altoona, PA and is the location of a source of dependably clean fresh water from a spring that erupts from the rocky ground there. The spring provides 8 million gallons of that water daily, so it was no wonder that a commercial enterprise dependent on that water would be located there.

The first of these was a grist mill located along what was the just called the Big Spring that originated in the 1760s. A small town grew up around the mill. Since the name of the family that owned the mill was Spang, it took no great leap of imagination to call the town Spang's Mills.

Since the spring produced those 8 millions gallons of water a day with a loud rushing sound, it also took no great leap of imagination to call the gusher Roaring Spring.

Then, along about 1867 a paper mill was built at the spring, taking advantage of that readily available clean water. The town that was already there consisting of a general store and a few homes, quickly exploded into a larger town to provide workers and ancillary services for the paper mill. That town became known as Roaring Spring, PA.

Over the years the town expanded, most of the millions of gallons of water from the Roaring Spring has been diverted for other usage, so it no longer roars. It is now enclosed within a stone arch and puts forth a murmur of water into Roaring Spring Dam Park, a small jewel of a man-made, crystal clear lake created to celebrate the Roaring Spring itself. The centerpiece of the park is a kaleidoscopic fountain that is illuminated by night.

Less noticeable is a nearby bridge and tunnel built near the old paper mill some years ago. It is unusual in that the bridge is completely enclosed by the tunnel and runs the length of it. It is also unusual in that it is haunted by the spirits of three people. One of those spirits is that of a man who had hanged himself, some people say from the bridge itself. He has been seen striding back and forth at the opposite end of the bridge from whichever end you are. His voice is also heard, but his words are never quite clear enough to decipher. He has reportedly even approached vehicles that stop on the bridge and thump on their windows with his hands.

Two other ghosts of the bridge are those of a pair of lovers who were struck and killed by a train above on the railroad overpass. They are seen walking along the length of the bridge, hand in hand, in love even after death.

A house of child-sacrificing, devil worship replete with cold spots frigid enough to produce icicles that hang from the ceilings of the rooms within is reputed to be nearby the bridge as well. Only problem is that nobody can ever find it, or any actual evidence that it ever existed. It seems to be one of those things that have always been witnessed by a friend of a friend.

All of these claims have been investigated by a number of groups, the most notable of which is the Paranormal Afterlife and Supernatural Team of Central Pennsylvania, which goes by the acronym PAST. Over the course of several visits to the site, PAST has encountered no unusual activity or sounds at the bridge. It doesn't mean there isn't any, it means that there is no scientific evidence of the hauntings.

Sometimes a Bargain Isn't

Huntington, PA

A fellow at a rural location related the following to me:

"I was building an addition to our house and needed some building materials. Not too far from me was a business that had been demolished after a nasty fire. The demolition contractor was selling various items that he had salvaged from the building. Things like doors, some windows, light fixtures, roof trusses and concrete blocks.

"It was the concrete blocks I needed and the price was right, about a fourth of what I'd pay for new blocks.

"When I brought the load home, a friend of mine cautioned me about them. He said that the original building burned down because it was cursed for being built over an Indian burial ground. And that the blocks may bring the curse with them.

"I just pooh-poohed that idea and went ahead with my addition, using the concrete blocks to make up the first story walls.

'Ever since I finished the project, it seems that a spirit has taken possession of the lower level of the addition and does anything he or she can do to irritate me, stuff like opening the basement door when nobody's home, stealing paper towels and scattering them on the floor, spilling small cans of paint – things like that."

He then asked me what he should do. I told him how to get in touch with a Native American shaman, explain his situation, and ask him if he could and would perform a purification rite to appease the spirits of the ancestors.

I gave the fellow my contact information, but I never learned how he handled his predicament.

Mr. Ed's Ghost

Ortanna, PA

Mr. Ed's Elephant Museum and Candy Emporium appears as an explosion of color along the Lincoln Highway when approaching Gettysburg from the west. Travelers from the west cannot count it as a trip to Gettysburg unless they stop in and say hi to Elly the elephant and enjoy the indoor and outdoor display of over 12,000 pachydermal figures of all sizes and shapes. Did I mention the candy? Candy, candy, candy of every kind – I once even saw beer-flavored jelly beans. And, can I mention the home-made fudge to die for that'll satisfy even the most discerning palate is made right there in the store by Cheryl, Mr. Ed's Chief Fudge Maker.

Is there actually a Mr. Ed? There sure is! Ed Gotwalt is the founder and patriarch of the business and has become a beloved Gettysburg celebrity. He is rightfully famous for his philanthropy, always giving back to the community. Mr. Ed sponsors free concerts and activities on-site weekly during the summer. His free 5,000-egg Easter egg hunt vies with his visit with Santa where each kid receives a free gift from the jolly old elf in popularity with area kids.

What's all this got to do with ghosts? Not much, unless you want to count the one that shares Mr. Ed's home with him.

For some reason or another, Mr. Ed and other members of his close-knit family smell the unmistakable aroma of Cherry pipe tobacco being smoked in his smoke-free home. Neither he nor any of his family members can recall anyone who actually smoked a pipe in the house.

Of course Gettysburg is known as one of the most haunted towns in all of the country. So, perhaps it is the spectre of a long departed Civil War soldier who had a particular penchant for cherry-flavored pipe tobacco. However, I don't know when cherry pipe tobacco was even developed, so it could just as easily be a farmer or townsman who passed on at some post-war year.

Who it might be is a matter of speculation and, until he makes an appearance, we can only guess from the not-unpleasant aroma of that sweet smelling pipe smoke.

ED KELEMEN

OK, Now I'm a Believer!

The Smoketown Inn

I had been exchanging pleasantries with a young lady who has spent at least as many decades on this planet as I when we switched the topic from the intricacies of flax scutching to health care. It seems as though people of our age are fascinated with anything that has to do with extending our lives.

All this talk of mortality naturally led to interacting with people who had already come to the end of their lives. Some people call them ghosts, others call them spirits. Whatever they are called, a lot of people refuse to acknowledge their existence. We've all heard variations of their denial time-after-time, usually stated thus: "There ain't no such things as ghosts!"

She introduced me to her husband of many years who confessed to being one of the nay-sayers when it came to ghosts. He said he was vociferous in his denial of the existence of an afterlife on this plane of existence. He had never seen a ghost, so they must not exist, right?

I had no desire to enter into a no-win conversation, so I just nodded my head. I wasn't agreeing with him, I was just acknowledging that I had heard him.

Then he said, "until," and I started paying attention again.

And here's the story of his conversion in his own words, starting with that attention grabbing word:

Until the wife and I stayed at a place near Lancaster, PA called the Smoketown Inn, room number seven, to be exact.

When we checked in, the desk clerk apologized, explaining that the only room left was number seven

I asked what was wrong with room number seven and was told nothing really, just that some people who stay there complain.

"About what?" I asked

"The ghosts," he replied.

"Yeah right," I told the clerk, "Just get us checked in. I'm sleepy."

Later that night, after the wife and I settled in, she poked me in the arm.

"Do you smell that? She asked.

"Smell what?"

"Horses," she replied.

Smell them I did. It wasn't overpowering. It was faint, as though a horse had been in the room some time ago and left a lingering odor. It wasn't even unpleasant to someone like me who grew upon a farm.

"I'll complain to the desk in the morning," I told her. And promptly forgot about it.

Later on she poked me again.

"Do you smell that?" she asked.

"Smell what."

"Horses."

"No," I told her.

"See?" She asked and rolled over and went to sleep.

The next day, Saturday, we made the obligatory tour of the Lancaster area Pennsylvania Dutch attractions. We ate at a humongous buffet, bought things that we would never have a use for, went for a hay ride, and "oohed and awed," at all the hex signs on the barns.

When we finally got back to the SmokeTown Inn after dark, we were ready for a hot shower and a night in the comfy bed. We were flat out exhausted and didn't even want a late night cocktail. So, we went to bed.

But not to sleep.

Someone was right outside the door to our room talking. Not loud enough to understand the words, but loud enough to interrupt our sleep. How rude! After a while, I got out of bed and went to the door. The talking went on and I yanked the door open to remonstrate them about their lack of courtesy. There was nobody there.

After looking up and down the hallway to be sure it was empty, I closed the door. The talking resumed and I yanked the door open again with the same results. On about the third, or maybe fourth time, the talking didn't stop. It went on in the hall outside the door with me standing there. But, just like the other times, I was the only one in the hall. I don't need to tell you, I was just a bit spooked.

I went back inside that room number seven and slammed the door hard enough to wake my wife, even though I didn't really mean to. She asked me what was going on.

After I told her, she said, "See?" then rolled over and went back to sleep.

But I didn't. Fully awake, I just lay there, staring at the dark ceiling and trying to make out the words in the spectral conversation just outside the door of our room.

Next thing was heavy footsteps clomping along the hallway. They always ended just outside the door to the room. Until the time they didn't.

I wasn't scared, just a bit annoyed with the prank being played on me.

Then the footsteps approached my door again. Only this time whoever it was walked right through the door and tromped into the room, ending right at the foot of our bed.

I saw the semi-solid apparition of a man dressed in the uniform of a Civil War soldier, but I couldn't tell whether it was a Confederate or Union uniform. The large, dirt covered man with the tangled beard pinned me in place with an evil stare that made me think *he* wanted *me* out of *his* room. And the definite aroma of a horse came right along with him. I remembered thinking that he should have at least had the common decency to scrape his boots before entering the room. That thought didn't last long. I was overcome with fear and reached over poking my wife until she awoke.

"Whaa...?" She mumbled, clearing the sleep from her eyes.

Then she saw the ghost at the foot of the bed. She sat up in the bed and we watched him as he faded away into nothingness.

I told my wife everything that happened leading up to the apparition walking through the door, arriving at the foot of the bed, then standing there in an accusatory manner.

She said, "And?"

I told her, "Honey, I've been wrong all these years! I'm sorry. I promise I'll never doubt you again."

She asked me, "Even the snow globe story?"

I replied, "Even the snow globe story."

Well, this got my attention again, so I asked, "what is the snow globe story?"

...And this brings us to our next, and final tale of the supernatural...

THE SNOWGLOBE
OF
DEATH

Central Pennsylvania Near Huntington

Now that her husband had admitted not only the possibility of, but the actual existence of an afterlife and other things beyond his immediate knowledge and without the presence of empirical proof, she told me the story of the snow globe.

In her own words -

When I was a young girl, I lived in the country. We had a small, bare existence farm. We were what you might call poor, but we didn't know it. Daddy worked at the mine when work was available and Mom made all our clothes. Granny did most of the cooking. The ground wasn't good enough for us to grow much more than just enough of a crop for ourselves, our chickens, and one nearly dry old cow.

The older folk along with my two sisters and I were all crammed into the old frame 2-story farm house on those few acres of hardscrabble land.

Granny sometimes got some money from folks for her curing and skrying. She had "the gift." People would come from all around the valley for Granny's help.

I guess that some people nowadays might call her a witch, but she wasn't. She just wanted to help people however she could. You see, she knew all about herbs and stuff like that.

When someone was having problems with their pregnancy, Granny was there to help with one of her potions. When that pregnancy came to term, she was always people's first choice as a midwife. She helped bring dozens of children into the world.

Nagging coughs, fever, stomach problems, headaches, woman's problems, sprains, strains, and what-have-you – Granny fixed 'em all. She could sew wounds and splint broken bones. That wasn't all, either.

Granny could "fix" other things as well. Young girls came to her for help in attracting true love and men came to her for help with nagging wives. Farmers asked her help with the weather for their crops, and couples asked for help with fertility.

Once in a while someone would ask for help with a particularly pesky problem. Like the farmer that complained that his neighbor was stealing some of his pigs and chickens. Mr. Halvorsen wanted the thief cursed, but Granny wouldn't do that. She never wanted to hurt anybody.

So she wrapped herself in a shawl, took a little bag of ingredients for her potions and went to the suspected thief's farm and had a visit.

While there, she mentioned that some pigs and chickens had recently turned up missing in the area and wanted to warn him and others about those animals in case they should wander onto their farms. Now, I don't know what, exactly, Granny told him about the animals. All I know is that about a week later Mr. Halvorsen stopped by with a fat piglet that he gave to Granny with his thanks for her help.

Now, all of Granny's efforts didn't have happy endings. Having the, "gift," she could sometimes see things that she rather wished she didn't. For instance, there was the young girl who found herself in the, "family way." Not only was she husband-less, she didn't even know who the father might be, although she had narrowed it down to two young fellows. She wanted Granny to name the father so that he could do the "right thing" by her.

Granny got out her skrying bowl, put some liquid in it along with a secret potion of hers. After lighting a candle, she then covered her head, the bowl, and the candle together under her shawl. She mumbled something in a sing-song voice while under there for what seemed an extraordinarily long time. Eventually, she uncovered herself, the bowl, and the candle announcing, "There's nothing I can do for you sweetie.

You lied to me."

Later that night I overheard my Mom and Granny talking. Mom said, "You know who the father is, don't you?"

Granny replied, "I do."

"Why then didn't you tell that poor girl?"

Granny said, "Oh that girl knows who it is. She lied when she swore that she had only been with two men who could have gotten her in that way."

Granny continued, "All I can say is that her baby is going to bear a mighty resemblance to her brother."

"I see," Mom said. It was never mentioned again.

Another time a couple brought a baby boy to Granny. It was a sickly little thing, definitely off its feed, coughing and feverish. They asked for Granny's help.

Granny wrapped the baby in her shawl and put it in the middle of Mom and Dad's bed. She sprinkled a little powder over it and said some prayers. Then, she asked to be alone with the baby for a while and we all left the room.

Ten or so minutes later and she came out of he bedroom, tears streaking her face.

"There's nothing I can do," she told the distraught parents. "It's beyond my abilities to help. Nature will run its course."

Then, we all said a prayer for the little one that its short time on this earth be without any more pain. But of course, it was. I think the prayer was more to make the little boy's parents feel better that it was for him.

One question they had for Granny was, "How long does our son have?"

"You have a snow globe on your mantle, don't you?" she asked.

"Why yes, but how did you know that?" the mother replied.

"It makes no difference how I know. Just know that that snow globe has a small leak in it. When all the water in it runs out, you son will no longer be with you."

And Granny would say no more.

A few months later, I found out that their baby had perished in early spring, just as the world was being reborn from its temporary winter death.

When the young couple returned to their home, the husband inspected the snow globe and found the teeny-tiny leak at the bottom. He figured that he could cheat Fate by sealing the leak, which he did with some pine rosin. And, it sat in its place of honor on the mantle leak free.

But, even though he was hanging on, their son deteriorated all through the winter. He was a pitiful little soul, in pain and crying a lot. When the weather started to change, he perked up a bit and they thought he was going to be fine. The little homestead was brightening after the long winter, just as nature itself was doing.

Then, one day in mid April, the wife heard the family dog going berserk out on the front porch. Running to see what was the matter, she opened the door and saw that the dog had cornered a squirrel where the porch roof meets the house.

"Stop it now, dog," she commanded. "He just a small fellow and not even worth shooting. Let him grow up and we'll eat him later."

With that, she shooed the dog away with her broom.

Just then, the squirrel clambered down the porch post and headed for his tree, but the dog saw him and lunged in his direction barking.

The squirrel darted through the opened door, the dog inches from its bushy tail, barking like there was no tomorrow.

She chased both of them, trying to corral the animals and get them out of the house, but they ran all over the first floor. The squirrel was adeptly running over, under, and around things without running into anything. The dog was another story. He ran into chairs, knocked stuff off the table, and caused chaos everywhere he went.

Finally, the squirrel lighted on the mantle and the young mother edged toward it, hoping to shoo it off and out the door. Just then the dog leaped for the squirrel, clearing off the mantle in the process.

The snow globe hit the floor, burst open and all its contents leaked out.

That night, the little baby boy, who had been baptized Lazarus, passed away.

You can't cheat Fate.

Years went by and Granny passed on. More years went by and Mom also passed on. They tried to teach me their ways, but either I was a lousy student or I just didn't have "the gift." But I do have some abilities to commune with spirits of folk who have left us for another realm of existence. Especially when I wear Granny's shawl.

About the Author

Ed Kelemen is an author, columnist, playwright and speaker who lives in a small west Central Pennsylvania town with two of his five sons, a huge dog, and a clutch of attitude ridden cats. His articles and short stories have appeared in numerous local, regional, and national publications. Visitors are always welcome at his website at www.ekelemen.com

Other Books by Ed Kelemen

All Titles Available at Amazon.com.

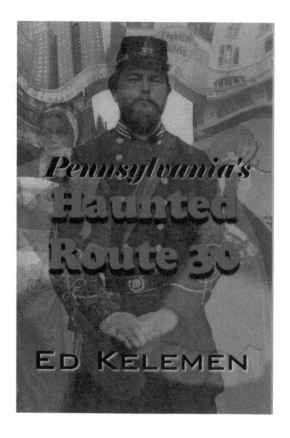

An East to West Haunted Tour along this historic highway visiting more than 55 of its most haunted places.

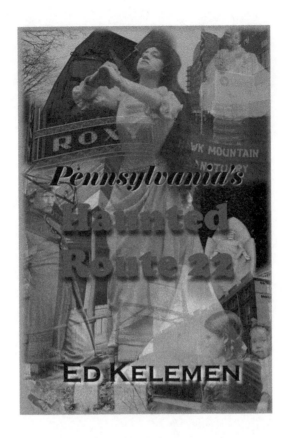

320 miles of haunted highway starting at Pittsburgh's Point State Park and ending at Stemie's Tavern in Easton, PA.

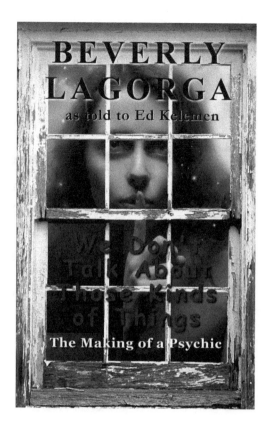

Join Beverly as she progresses from a frightened little girl of eight years to a woman who both realizes and develops her psychic ability so that she can help others.

Abagail died a hero on the blood-soaked battlefield of Gettysburg, but was denied a soldier's grave.

Now her spirit roams that battlefield seeking justice before it is too late.

Bert, Emma, Ronnie, and Derek, just a bunch of kids on vacation, risk all to help her get the hero's burial she deserves before time runs out.

A gentle ghost story for young and young at heart readers.

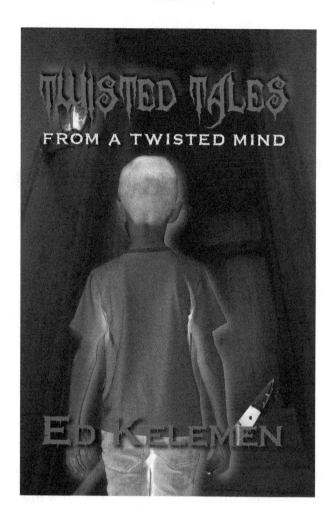

A fiendishly delicious collection of creepy stories.